THE GOLDEN CONSTANT

THE GOLDEN CONSTANT

AMERICAN INSTITUTE FOR ECONOMIC RESEARCH:
75 YEARS OF FREE THINKING ON THE FREE MARKET (1933–2008)

EDITED BY FREDERICK C. HARWOOD
AND CHARLES MURRAY

American Institute for Economic Research, P.O. Box 1000, Great Barrington, MA 01230

www.aier.org

Library of Congress Control No.: 2008933661

ISBN: 978-0-913610-62-6

Executive editor: Frederick C. Harwood, Trustee, AIER

Coeditor: Charles Murray, President and CEO, AIER

Writer: Michael Sion, mikewriter38@earthlink.net

Page designer: Milan Sperka, www.meshcreative.com

Printer: Sheridan Books, Chelsea, Michigan

First edition

Published in the United States of America

TABLE OF CONTENTS

Acknowledgments IX

Introduction — AIER Reaches 75: Carrying Forth the Vision of Its Founder XI

Chapter One — The 1930s: In the Depths of the Depression, AIER Is Born 1

Chapter Two — The 1940s: After War's Interruption, AIER Finds a Perfect Campus 15

Chapter Three — The 1950s: Postwar Expansion and Cold War Politics 33

Chapter Four — The 1960s: A Decade of Turbulence; the Colonel vs. Uncle Sam. 41

Chapter Five — The 1970s: Stagflation and Inflation; AIER Outlasts the SEC 53

Chapter Six — The 1980s: Reaganomics, Market Crash; Life without the Colonel 75

Chapter Seven — The 1990s: Bull Market and High-tech Bubble; AIER Nurtures Sound Scholars . . 85

Chapter Eight — The 2000s: New Millennium with Old Problems; AIER Reaches New Markets. . . 103

Conclusion — Toward the Next 75 Years 129

Appendix A — A Leading Publisher of Economic Education 133

Appendix B — Charitable Giving Sustains AIER 137

Appendix C — The Free-flowing Pen of E.C. Harwood: Three Essays 143

Appendix D — How to Contact AIER 157

Photo Index 159

Subject Index 163

To the cumulative millions of book buyers, members, and contributors,

the Institute's lifeblood since 1933.

ACKNOWLEDGMENTS

The editors thank the many people who participated in the research and production of this 75th anniversary book for the American Institute for Economic Research. These include individuals who gave their time to relate their experiences with the Institute: William Ford, Maureen Foulke, Bruce Gore, Christa Jensen, Kerry Lynch, Lawrence Pratt, Elaine Tan, Walker Todd, Robert C. Weems, and Jean White.

Many other Institute staffers and associates also contributed to the production of this book. Among them were Ryan Goodenough, who provided input on the cover design, and Marcia Stamell, who proofread the manuscript. Katy Delay and Michelle Harwood read an early draft of the manuscript. Michael Sion researched, organized and wrote the text. Milan Sperka designed the pages and covers.

Last but not least, the Institute's Board of Trustees provided invaluable support and encouragement, without which this book would not have been possible.

INTRODUCTION

E.C. Harwood, yearbook photo, U.S. Military Academy, West Point, New York, 1920.

The year 2008 marks the 75th anniversary of the founding of the American Institute for Economic Research — an organization standing peerless among think tanks and public-interest research groups. AIER's journey has proved to be as remarkable as it has been improbable. From modest beginnings, in the depths of the Great Depression in borrowed office space on a college campus, funded by $200 scraped together by a young founder who squeezed in time to write the Institute's books and newsletters and court subscribers while fulfilling a full-time Army position, AIER has defied conventional wisdom both in its uncompromisingly objective research — and in its very survival.

"Any economist will say that what we're trying to do will not work," noted Charles Murray, AIER president and CEO, as the 75th anniversary approached. "But we've got the contrapositive. We're here, and we're thriving. That's so characteristic of AIER. The evidence is contrary to what the theory would tell you."

What distinguishes AIER from other economic research groups is its absolute devotion to purely objective financial research uncompromised by governmental grants, large corporate donations, or gifts from special interests with strings attached. Similarly, the Institute has no commercial connection with any outside enterprise. Its publications do not carry advertising of any sort. Its bylaws prohibit seeking and maintaining a large endowment; the funds the Institute receives must be expended solely for Institute purposes, and within a reasonable time after receipt.

From its organization in 1933 by its iconoclastic, self-educated founder, E.C.

Harwood, as a private and independent, scientific and educational charitable organization, AIER's two-fold mission has never wavered — to produce fact-based research to help individual Americans protect their personal financial interests; and to indirectly influence federal policy, through dissemination of the Institute's unbiased research, to fight inflation and maintain price stability and the dollar's strength.

Fittingly, the Institute lives or dies by the market; that is, the Institute's existence depends upon the merits of its work. If the research and analysis prove faulty, or the financial advice of no avail, its readers and subscribers will vanish. Thus, the Institute naturally avoids the "ivory tower" syndrome of producing research for research's sake, never mind the results. AIER produces useful, low-cost information about financial matters of genuine importance to individuals.

What's more, the scientific research methods AIER has refined over the decades — including its development of primary leading, coincident and lagging statistical indicators — often has yielded findings that anticipated "popular

1926: The cover of *Life* showing a flapper doing the Charleston with an older man of means.

wisdom" by months or even years. In summer 2007, AIER researchers explained the nation was close to a recession — a full half-year before popular media reported this reality. More significantly, AIER warned of the impending crises in Social Security and Medicare before these programs became law. AIER's sustaining members, however, were apprised of such information long before the masses, via the Institute's twice-monthly Research Reports *and monthly* Economic Education Bulletins.

Along the way to its diamond anniversary, AIER has withstood many challenges and battles — from growing pains characteristic of any organization, to investigations by the Internal Revenue Service, to legal attacks by the Securities and Exchange Commission alleging infractions of investment law. Lean years and an uncertain future plagued the Institute's stalwarts,

Automobiles symbolized both newfound wealth and Americans' increasing mobility.

but the storms inevitably passed. And today — in the first decade of a new century — AIER continues to grow in membership and reserves, to expand its conferences and fellowship programs for established and budding economists, and to chart new markets and methods by which to disseminate its research and educational tools in the diverse, fast-paced society of today's America.

AIER's history is inextricably tied to the life of its inimitable founder, Col. Edward Crosby Harwood. Therefore, the story of the Institute properly follows, to a large degree, Harwood's own story, up to the time of his passing in 1980. His unwavering vision and his steadfast efforts in building and preserving AIER created a legacy that is very real: the thriving Institute we know today.

We turn now to the decade leading up to that of the Great Depression of the 1930s —"The Roaring Twenties." It was during this period when a young E.C. Harwood entered adulthood, embarked on an exhaustive personal study of economics — and began prodigiously penning and publishing articles predicting impending financial gloom.

THE 1920S ROAR . . . BUT END IN A WHIMPER

A ZEITGEIST OF PROSPERITY and modernization prevailed in America during the Roaring Twenties, the decade following the Great War. This was the age of hot jazz and speakeasies, larger-than-life athletes such as Babe Ruth and Jack Dempsey, "talkie" motion pictures and Charles Lindbergh's solo flight across the Atlantic. The burgeoning electric-power industry transformed everyday living, with power lines and telephone lines reaching the countryside. Factory assembly lines mass-produced radios, household appliances and Model T Fords for a nation rapidly urbanizing and expanding its spidering network of roads.

The heady spirit of optimism fueled consumer consumption. Department stores and oil companies offered credit cards for the first time. Stock-market investment caught the fancy not only of wealthy Americans but also of those in the middle class, who came to regard retail brokerages, and securities affiliates of commercial banks, as safe places through which to invest. Speculative euphoria fueled an historic expansion of the stock market. Corporations introduced new security issues, particularly in preferred and common stock. Banks offered not only mortgages and installment loans, but also loans to securities speculators on 90 percent margins. Banks themselves gambled on land development. About 1 in 10 U.S. households owned stocks.

On Aug. 24, 1921, the Dow Jones Industrial Average finished at 63.90 points. Eight years later, the Dow had increased nearly 600 percent, closing on Sept. 3, 1929, at a high-water mark: 381.17. Two months later, though, investors' panic set in when the artificially inflated stock values triggered a massive sell-off. On Oct. 28 — "Black Monday" — the Dow dropped nearly 13 percent, and the following day fell another 12 percent. No rally ensued. The crash triggered widespread bank failures. Public faith in government and business plunged. The prolonged economic contraction that became known as "The Great Depression" set in.

Had warning signals of this impending financial doom been recognized? Indeed they had, in the eyes of a young, independent scholar of economics. His name: Edward Crosby Harwood. His academic pedigree was highly unusual for the field. Similarly, his views diverged significantly from his fellow economists. In fact, his entire background showed him to be a most singular, freethinking individual.

A SOLDIER STEEPS HIMSELF IN ECONOMIC TEXTS — AND GOES TO BATTLE AGAINST PREVAILING FINANCIAL PUNDITRY

BORN INTO A WORKING-class family in Cliftondale, Massachusetts, on Oct. 28, 1900, Edward Harwood proved to be a top scholar in high school and an ambitious young man eager to better himself by attending college. With no parental support to pursue higher education, he managed to earn an appointment to the United States Military Academy at West Point, New York, from which he graduated, 10th in his class, in 1920. He added a civil engineering degree from Rensselaer Polytechnic Institute, in Troy, New York, in 1922, and served as a second lieutenant in the U.S. Army Corps of Engineers.

But it was a different field — economics — that caught his interest as an intellectual avocation. Money-credit problems especially engaged his restless mind as an area of study. He began writing freelance magazine articles on this subject. But a deeper education lay in store for him. Harwood would later say of this period: "After writing articles published in leading journals from 1923 to 1926, without benefit of academic training in economics, I was transferred to Hawaii where thousands of books collected during the World War I book drives had been sent and placed in a large library. Among them, arranged by author alphabetically, were

"In our view, the most innovative and successful social order to date has been that based on individual sovereignty, which began to evolve in late medieval England. The development of English Common Law, especially Magna Carta and the termination of Star Chamber proceedings, greatly advanced the rights of persons to be secure in their persons and possessions. However, the most significant subsequent experiment was the Constitution of the United States, especially its Bill of Rights. In addition to limiting the power of government by the express enumeration of Federal responsibilities, the U.S. Constitution affirms the basic Common Law rights of each person to freedom from coercion by others, and embraces the fundamental dictum of equity justice that no one has a right to take without compensation the fruits of another's effort."

— *AIER After 70 Years, Our History and Plans for the Future* hundreds of books on economics and philosophy, including practically all that had been published in the preceding several decades.

"In the absence of formal guidance, I began with the A's and continued toward the end of the alphabet. After reading only a few, I found a bewildering divergence of views clearly traceable to almost incredibly slipshod use of technical terms and numerous errors in simple logic. Fairly early in the search I found a set of books written by Henry George about 40 years earlier. In these there was the painstaking application of technical names or terms that I had been taught in the physical sciences, as well as logical exposition that contrasted markedly with the other hundreds of books on economics.

"Until I had read George's work I had begun to doubt my judgment about the others. How could so many supposedly learned professors be in error repeatedly; was there something wrong about my analyses of their writings; were the logic and the procedures of inquiry I had learned at West Point not applicable in the field of economics? Although I continued, somewhat bewildered, to the end of the alphabet, I could find no evidence of improvement. By that time I was seriously questioning, How do I know that I know anything?

"Also in the library were several shelves of books on philosophy, including advanced logic. I had understood that a branch of philosophy designated epistemology presumably provided the answer to my question. Therefore I began with the A's on the philosophy shelves to seek the elusive answer. Within a few months I

Portrait of American philosopher, psychologist and educator William James (1842 - 1910). His works influenced young E.C. Harwood.

discovered that the answer was not there, or at least I could not find it. The situation there was as bad, perhaps worse, than that in economics. However, I also found a glimmer of light, or what seemed to me possible approaches toward the light, in some writings of William James. Several years later, as I followed the writings of John Dewey and Arthur Bentley in the philosophical quarterlies, I was to learn that James and Dewey had indeed been on the path toward an answer to my question."

Armed with the ability to clearly and critically analyze financial data, Harwood continued writing articles that were printed in leading journals of the day, including *Barron's* and *Bankers Magazine*. In several articles widely published in 1928 and 1929, he predicted the coming depression, which he blamed on the inordinate issuances of corporate securities, and on the vast amounts of loans by financial institutions to investors and speculators fueling the stock-market boom. Harwood labeled these practices "the great inflating via over-expansion of private credit extensions."

To aid his research, he developed a procedure — an "Index of Inflating" — for estimating the amount of purchasing media in use, in relation to that needed. Harwood held that when excess purchasing media were created, inflating had occurred. He traced the trend to the U.S. government's inflating the currency, in lieu of instituting a tax, to fund America's war effort in Europe in 1917 and 1918. He attributed much of the boom of the Roaring Twenties to that bubble, and to follow-on policies by the government to goose the economy after the war boom. He recognized that the process of inflating was a backdoor theft, a regressive one, which invisibly picked people's pockets.

Using banking data, Harwood concluded that in 1929, inflating was taking place at a rapid rate in spite of comparative stability of the popular price indexes. The excesses of inflating could be found, he said, in limited areas of the economy, particular in the stock market and in real estate. Paper profits from investments in securities and real property had spurred spending on consumer goods, which led to overall robust business activity. Yet, Harwood asserted, the excesses of inflating eventually would lead to a recession.

> **"**Any economist will say that what we're trying to do will not work. But we've got the contrapositive. We're here, and we're thriving. That's so characteristic of AIER. The evidence is contrary to what the theory would tell you.**"**
>
> *— Charles Murray, AIER president and CEO*

His articles caught the eyes of influential businessmen and academicians. His reputation continued to grow after his forecasts were proved accurate by the drastic contraction in the nation's economy that began in late 1929. And in 1933, as America gloomily sat in a deep depression, a top administrator at the Massachusetts Institute of Technology encouraged Harwood, then an assistant professor of military science and training on the campus, to initiate a research organization to provide valuable financial advice to ordinary citizens and to determine the causes and potential cures for the economic sinkhole in which the nation had plunged.

With $200 saved up from selling his articles, and free use of cramped office space and the campus's mailing department, Harwood juggled his work schedule, hired a couple of clerical assistants, and founded the American Institute for Economic Research. ❖

A PLUCKY SPIRIT AND EAGER INTELLECT LIFT AN AMBITIOUS LAD OUT OF A MODEST HOME — AND LAUNCH HIM TOWARD GREAT HORIZONS

From an early age, Edward Crosby Harwood saw that if he were to rise above the modest means of his household and make his mark in the world, he would have to do so under his own steam. To his good fortune, a rare ambition burned in this oldest of three sons and a daughter growing up in Longmeadow, Massachusetts, near Springfield, in the first two decades of the 20th century.

Edward Crosby's father, Edward Thomas Harwood, although hard working, had never enjoyed much personal opportunity. He had emigrated from London, England, at age 5 in 1871 with his mother and three younger siblings, joining his father, Edward J. Harwood, who'd already arrived in Springfield. They were late in the wave of Harwoods, who'd been emigrating from England to America, beginning with colonial Virginia, since the 1600s. Two more children were born to Edward J's. family, who subsisted near the poverty

Edward Harwood, age 3, Cliftondale, Massachusetts. With toy shovel and pail — already exhibiting a work ethic.

level because of his alcoholism. Edward Thomas, in fact, quit school in the ninth grade and became the family's main breadwinner, toiling as a stock boy at a department store. Though intelligent, industrious and honest, he never found an occupation that would provide his own family with a comfortable life. Complicating his financial position, the woman he married — Mary Howe Pinney, the daughter of a prosperous butcher and town alderman who was descended from a Connecticut pioneer family — had delusions of living a life of splendor. That further strained the welfare of the household of five.

Edward Crosby, born Oct. 28, 1900, in Cliftondale, north of Boston, could not suppress his childhood appetite for youthful necessities such as roller skates and a bicycle, despite his family's meager means. His father became a baker at a large bakery in Longmeadow, where the family settled, but his wages left little for leisure spending. That didn't deter his eldest child. He possessed an unusually high energy level and active mind. As resourceful as he was ambitious, at age 10 Edward Crosby took a newspaper route. Making money filled him with pride — and nourished dreams. By the time he'd progressed to distributing *Saturday Evening Post* and *Country Gentleman* magazines, his work ethic was well honed and he continuously increased his territory. The Curtis Publishing Company held a contest for the most copies sold, offering cash prizes on a weekly cumulative basis. Edward, now yearning to save for a college education, set a national record for selling copies. He kept his savings in a bank account. And his busy mind churned out new ideas for generating revenue.

The teenaged Edward continued building up his savings by cleaning out neighborhood cellars and attics. This labor was dirty and physically demanding. The typical cellar in 1918 was filled with huge tubs of coal cinders and ashes by the time spring came around after a cold winter. But young Ed Harwood, wiry and standing a couple inches under 6 feet, was more than willing to tackle the task. His mind proved as valuable an asset as his muscles. As Harwood's second wife, Helen Fowle Harwood, would later write in an article, "A talent for discerning more efficient ways to operate served him well."

The city of Springfield provided free refuse collection, with trucks hauling away trash put out in barrels on the sidewalk. "In a preliminary survey of one early job, a charnel house of a cellar," Helen wrote, "Ed was dismayed to find only two barrels available. Several times that many would be needed in which to stash the discards. The two additional barrels that he was able to cadge from home still would permit only four barrels to be put out at one time, but having to spend several days on a single job was displeasing to one already precociously aware of the value of time.

"The solution that he came up with would not have appealed to a more experienced youngster. Fortunately, the city collected on Saturdays. Always up early, it was no problem for Ed to have the four barrels filled and lined up on the sidewalk well ahead of collection. As fast as the two men on the truck emptied a barrel, Ed whisked it back into the cellar for refilling. Intelligence not being a requisite for their job, the men were slow to catch on. When it dawned on them why they never seemed to exhaust the line of barrels coming out of the cellar, they were at first annoyed. Then the ingenuity of a plucky kid tickled them. They made a game of it, speeding up or slowing down in an attempt to catch him flat-footed. But Herculean effort enabled Ed to keep on track, and the crew

Lt. Ed Harwood, (first) wife, Harriet, and daughter, Midge, Hawaii, 1926.

E.C. Harwood (front, center) with fellow student leaders, Technical High School, Springfield, Massachusetts, 1918.

drove off, heads shaking in disbelief. Ed collapsed on the bare floor of the cellar, but another worthwhile sum went toward the college education becoming a probability."

His status-conscious mother, however, had other ideas for her son's hard-earned savings: financing the purchase of a larger house for the family. Toward this end, and with no opposition from her cowed husband, she drained Edward's account, which he, being a minor, could not prevent. He absorbed the blow in stride, considered his options, and resolved that his stellar high school grades would earn him a scholarship to the state university at Amherst, where he could study agriculture in preparation of becoming a successful farmer.

Edward's proclivity toward independent thinking manifested itself not only in plotting his academic and professional future, but in his approach to religion. Although raised in the Congregational Church, by 17 he was following his own path. As he recalled in an essay written at age 73, "I began to discard all religious affiliations, a process that was completed a few years later. This does not mean that I am an atheist, because an atheist claims that there is no God, whereas I do not claim to know anything about such matters. Nor do I consider myself an agnostic, because an agnostic claims that anything outside the realm of material things cannot be known. I do not feel in a position to make such an assertion."

Fate interrupted Edward's plans to attend college at Amherst. The United States, in 1917, entered the Great War. Grade skipping had left Edward younger than his classmates, but he was a leader among his peers, who had elected him president of their graduating class at Technical High School in Springfield. He considered enlisting in the military along with his fellow male seniors. But another opportunity for him appeared, and rather miraculously. The first candidate for the local U.S. congressional appointment in 1918 to the U.S. Military Academy had a broken arm and failed his physical examination. The anxious congressman from Springfield's district asked the high school principal to recommend a substitute. The principal's decision was easy: honor student E.C. Harwood. The hard labor of cleaning cellars over the years allowed him easily to pass the Army physical, and Edward was admitted to West Point.

He would prove to be the only one of his parents' children to rise far above their working-class home. Brothers Harry and William went into the trades; sister Doris became a school music teacher. As Helen Harwood would one day remark while assessing her husband's clamber up the socioeconomic ladder, "He was a freak." Through sheer hard work and unbridled drive, E.C. Harwood had broken from the mold.

A FAMILY, A HAWAII POSTING, A PERSONAL QUEST FOR FINANCIAL EXPERTISE

THE WARTIME DEMAND FOR well-trained officers shortened the academic period for graduation at West Point to two years. Edward finished 10th in the Class of 1920, and joined the Army's Corps of Engineers. The war was over by now, leaving a glut of lieutenants. Edward married his high school sweetheart, Harriet Haynes, in 1921, with whom he would have two sons and a daughter. In 1922, he earned his master's in civil engineering from Rensselaer Polytechnic Institute. He began studying economics on his own and penning freelance articles— a pastime that accelerated with earnest after the Army transferred him to the Schofield Barracks Army installation on the island of Oahu, Hawaii, in 1926.

Other young Army officers in his situation fell into lives of slow dissipation, turning to drink or chasing women. But Lt. Harwood, a husband and father, directed his idle time toward pursuing an intellectual interest — the study of economics, and particularly money-credit problems. What fueled his interest were his hours browsing the stacks in the extensive collection of books on economics in the Schofield Barracks Library — whose shelves had been stocked by citizens' donations during the Great War of the previous decade. The collection of tomes represented nearly every title on the subject published in the preceding decades, and the young officer resolved to read every one, progressing alphabetically by authors' names. Soon, his scientifically trained mind was recoiling at the imprecise language and logical fallacies he encountered among the widely differing views of the authors.

Harwood's salvation, of a sort, came after he hit the G's. Henry George's book, *Progress and Poverty*, offered coherence amid the chaotic tangle of opinions in the other books. George wrote with clear exposition and careful application of technical terms. Having exhausted the collection of economics books, Harwood burned with a very basic philosophical question — in his words, "How do I know that I know anything?"

He turned next to the library's section of philosophy books, including on advanced logic. As with the economics books, the voraciously inquisitive autodidact encountered a muddle of ideas and terminology. To his relief, he discovered that John Dewey and William James were

Lt. E.C. Harwood and horse (who wears the hat), Hawaii.

solid islands in the semantic swamp, clarifying a murky bog of philosophical issues. Harwood believed that, just as in the physical sciences, the behavioral aspects of economics could be studied using rigid scientific methodology. He began applying scientific methods to see if he could determine what caused the booms and busts in the business cycle. Ironically, he was a low-paid soldier who couldn't consider investing any of his meager salary, were he to find a suitable investment. Yet he was developing a deep understanding of financial currents.

Harwood continued researching money-credit matters and landing articles in such prestigious publications as the *New York Times*, *Barron's* and *Banker's Magazine*. In several articles printed in 1928 and 1929, he predicted a coming economic depression — ascribing the incipient crisis to a disastrous inflation of the monetary supply from an overabundance of purchasing media such as corporate securities, and bank loans to investors and speculators. While Americans were savoring a prolonged stock-market boom, Lt. E.C. Harwood was sounding an alarm.

Harwood's marriage did not last. Life in Hawaii did not suit Harriet, and she returned to the mainland with the children: Midge, Ted and Richard. Harwood himself returned to the states in 1929, after the Army transferred him to Rensselaer Polytechnic Institute, in Troy, New York, where he had earned a bachelor's degree in civil engineering. Now he added a master's degree in that field. An assignment the following year placed him at the Massachusetts Institute of Technology, where he took the opportunity to obtain a master's degree of business administration with formal requirements in economics. Now he had academic training to augment his independent scholarship.

By now, Harwood's well-researched, flawlessly reasoned essays were drawing the attention of some prominent people in academia and the business world. In a few years, some of the people he impressed would offer him an opportunity to apply his well-developed critical skills and acumen to economic research meant to save the nation

CHAPTER ONE
THE 1930S:
IN THE DEPTHS OF THE DEPRESSION, AIER IS BORN

When Franklin Delano Roosevelt was inaugurated as the 32nd U.S. president on March 4, 1933, the nation was in the depths of its worst depression. The images from this era are of haggard Okies and Arkies in ramshackle jalopies loaded to the brim, rumbling west to the putative promised land of California; of soup lines and hobo camps; of "Red" labor agitators preaching revolution; of muffin-faced young men far from home, toiling on government-funded work crews constructing roads and dams.

Roosevelt's predecessor, Herbert Hoover, had drastically raised taxes to boost declining federal revenues, and passed the protectionist Smoot-Hawley Tariff — which boomeranged on the U.S. economy after retaliatory moves by foreign trading partners. Now, one out of every four U.S. workers was unemployed. Two million Americans were homeless. National income was 50 percent below the 1929 average. Farm prices had plunged 60 percent, and industrial production had plummeted by more than half since 1929. Tens of thousands of impoverished families migrated from the Midwest to California, seeking better lives. Bank runs were common, and 32 of the 48 states had closed their banks. The

Dow Jones Industrial Average had lost about 85 percent of its value since the Depression's onset. The interest rate on U.S. Treasury bills had gone negative, since investors were amenable to taking a loss just to know their money was secure. With the money supply shrunk by a third, barter had become increasingly common.

Roosevelt, in his inaugural address, blamed the economic crisis on bankers, brokers, financiers — and the profit motive itself. "Rulers of the exchange of mankind's goods," the new

President Franklin D. Roosevelt initiated large federal relief programs.

A line of hungry men wait to enter the Municipal Lodging House in New York, for a free meal. "Soup lines" were common in the 1930s.

president declared with charismatic conviction, "have failed through their own stubbornness and their own incompetence, have admitted their failure, and have abdicated. Practices of the unscrupulous money changers stand indicted in the court of public opinion, rejected by the hearts and minds of men. True they have tried, but their efforts have been cast in the pattern of an outworn tradition. Faced by failure of credit they have proposed only the lending of more money." Roosevelt struck a rhetorical chord for intensive governmental intervention: "The money changers have fled from their high seats in the temple of our civilization. We may now restore that temple to the ancient truths. The measure of the restoration lies in the extent to which we apply social values more noble than mere monetary profit."

Roosevelt's advisers prepared a legislative agenda to boost the economy through strengthening the banking system, reforming the stock market and providing relief to the unemployed. With avuncular magnetism, FDR spelled out his "New Deal" in his "fireside chat" radio addresses. He signed the Securities Act, requiring strong disclosure statements of publicly held corporations; the Banking Act, creating the Federal Deposit Insurance Corporation; and the Securities Exchange Act, forming the

Bank run, 1929: Investors rushing to withdraw their savings following the stock-market crash.

Securities and Exchange Commission. He initiated dozens of relief programs, funding his emergency budget with debt. Among these "alphabet agencies" were the CCC (Civilian Conservation Corps), WPA (Works Progress Administration), TVA (Tennessee Valley Authority), and FHA (Federal Housing Administration). FDR, as the president was popularly called, also signed into law the Federal Insurance Contributions Act — creating the Social Security system, funded by dedicated payroll taxes, to provide pensions to aged retirees, survivors of deceased workers, disabled workers and the unemployed.

Roosevelt also took radical action to address what his advisers said were a problem of low prices. He devalued the U.S. dollar in 1934 by raising its price from $20.67 to $35 per ounce

of gold. He also ordered that all gold held by Americans be confiscated by the government, at the previous exchange rate — thereby giving the government a paper profit on the rise in the price of gold.

The economic effects of the Roosevelt's policies were debatable. By 1936, the gross domestic product had climbed by 34 percent over its 1932 level, but unemployment was still above 9 percent. The president declared that a third of Americans remained poorly fed, housed and clothed. What's more, a new recession struck in 1937. As history records, it would take a major war to fully lift the nation out of the economic contraction.

AN INDEPENDENT SCHOLAR PREDICTS AN IMPENDING DEPRESSION

THE GREAT DEPRESSION MAY have caught a nation and its leaders by surprise, but at least one scholar had seen the crisis coming: a young Army officer named Edward C. Harwood. His college degree was in civil engineering, and he was a rare bird among financial thinkers: a self-taught economist who prolifically penned articles published in leading journals in the field. As Harwood would later write of this period: " . . . the great inflating via over-expansion of private credit extensions was spiraling upward with the reckless abandon of a burgeoning speculative mania toward the 1929 disaster. As it happened, I had developed a procedure for measuring the extent of the inflating and its gradual approach to the unyielding limits provided, fortunately, by

American scientist, inventor and college administrator Vannevar Bush (1890-1974) supported AIER's founding. Bush's "differential analyser" was a forerunner of the computer.

the remnant of the gold standard, that is, by the gold-exchange monetary standard. In several articles during 1928 and 1929 published in leading journals, the progress (if it can be called that) of continued inflating was measured, and finally in the summer of 1929 imminent termination of the process was emphasized."

In 1929, the Army transferred Harwood to Rennselaer Polytechnic Institute, in New York state, for a second period of graduate study. He earned a master's degree in civil engineering. The following year he took an assignment as an associate professor of military science and training at Massachusetts Institute of Technology, and added a degree in business administration with formal requirements in economics. Although Harwood had dutifully carried out Army Corps of Engineer assignments supervising construction projects for the federal Works Progress Administration and Civilian Conservation Corps — and applying his prodigious skill for seeing the big picture of a project by planning out sites in the Northeast region for the CCC camps — he cast a doubtful eye on a federal plan to boost the economy by increasing these projects. Harwood wrote:

"When the lean year came the administration in Washington called a conference at which new construction pledges were made. Railroads, utilities, states and municipalities, and, of course, the federal government, all agreed to increase construction in order to bring back the days of the full dinner pail. For a time the vast undertakings initiated in accordance with the pledges made in Washington seemed to exert a steadying influence. During the early spring of 1930 many observers apparently believed that the depression was over. But the *Index of Inflating* told a different story."

Harwood advanced his view on the failure of the federal construction program in an article published in May 1930, writing it at a time he noted was, "just when it seemed most certain to many that the corner had been turned." As Harwood would recall years later, similar articles he penned caught the eyes of a number of businessmen, as well as a U.S. senator, who had written to Harwood at length in 1932 to urge "that I serve as head of a new economic research

> 66 The truth of the matter is that we (citizens of voting age today) are attempting to provide for our own old age at the expense of our children and grandchildren. We would not dream of assuming one-third of the burden that we are planning to place on the shoulders of those too young to know what we are doing, and others yet unborn. . . . We are assuming that our children and grandchildren will be peculiarly eager to shoulder burdens which were not of their making. 99
>
> — *"Whither Social Security?,"* AIER Weekly Bulletin, Jan. 23, 1939

organization to be known as The Committee for Economic Development. They planned to obtain donations totaling millions of dollars, and they hoped that within six months the new organization would provide useful answers to the nation's economic problems. Although I was pleased with the confidence thus indicated in my writings, I felt obliged to point out that not six months but probably at least a quarter century would be required, because a new generation of economists would be needed who had learned more useful procedures of inquiry. The eager seekers for a quick solution found another individual to head the proposed organization. Nearly 50 years later it still has not found the desired solution for the nation's economic problems. Obviously, I was overoptimistic in my estimate of a quarter century."

A FARSIGHTED SUPPORTER AT MIT SPURS AIER'S FOUNDING

ANOTHER INFLUENTIAL PERSON HAD seen the wisdom of starting a think tank, to be headed by Lt. Harwood, to research the causes of the Great Depression and produce economic policy recommendations. This person was Vannevar Bush, dean of the Massachusetts Institute of Technology. (Such was Bush's visionary power, that he later established the military/university research partnership that developed the ARPANET — forerunner to the Internet.) Bush had read Harwood's book, published in 1932, *Cause and Control of the Business Cycle*, which had grown out of Harwood's research and copious writing of

financial articles. Bush suggested that a research organization to be created could support itself by selling publications intended to help individuals seeking to resolve their personal financial woes. As a nonprofit organization, it also could survive with small annual contributions from thousands of individuals — saving it the risk of having its research and results compromised by the views of one or a few wealthy donors, or of a conventional endowment fund.

Harwood already occupied a professor's office at MIT. Dean Bush agreed to let Harwood use that space for conducting basic economic research, and to use the college's mail services. Harwood budgeted a half workday to his Army officer duties and the remaining time to the new enterprise. He scraped together $200 from his freelance article income, and printed advertising circulars offering for sale a $1 booklet (yet to be written) on what inflation meant to the average citizen. He hired two young women at low wages to type and stuff envelopes and perform other secretarial work. One was Gertrude Bedrick, a recent graduate of Simmons College. The other: Helen Longfellow Fowle, who had been a sports reporter for the *Boston Globe*, paid by the column inch as a "stringer."

Lo and behold — $1 bills began coming to the office from subscribers, and Harwood wrote the 64-page booklet, *What Will Devaluation Mean to You?* Harwood took no salary from AIER, surviving instead on his military pay. As the Institute's work volume grew, young women with college degrees hard-pressed to find more remunerative employment typed and stuffed envelopes for $12 a week. In 1934, AIER formally associated.

From its start, the Institute set up a structure to preserve its absolute intellectual freedom by refusing to seek support from charitable foundations, wealthy business interests or governmental agencies that could very well attach strings to financial aid. The Institute's first *Research Reports* publication, in November 1934, began: "This organization judges, not men, but the effects of the acts of men. We must concentrate attention on the results to be expected, ignoring the intent of the individuals involved. What men hope for and intend to achieve furnishes a clue to their characters, but . . . the means chosen by which we will carry out these intentions must have concrete results."

AIER's staff grew to six. Subscriptions steadily built, and the volume of correspondence overburdened MIT's mail facility. MIT president Karl T. Compton ordered that Harwood would have to find other quarters for his institute. He and Helen found a small apartment to rent in Cambridge, near Harvard Square, at $40 a month, and furnished it with furniture and typewriters purchased at bargain rates from the Harvard Economic Society, which Helen later wrote "had gone broke giving lousy advice to clients and was selling office equipment." The Institute eventually moved into a larger apartment in the building at $50 a month, as AIER's business operations continued to expand, including from the launch of a bimonthly set of bulletins offering investment advice. Harwood recommended buying defaulted bonds that were selling for 10 cents or so on the dollar, but which he said would eventually regain their values. (They did.)

Lt. Harwood, meanwhile, was busy in his regular career. The Army assigned him as executive officer of the widening of the Cape Cod Canal and overseer of the Corp of Engineers' Massachusetts Flood Control Program. His engineering studies proving no need for locks on the canal saved millions of dollars on the project, and in 1935 won him a prize from the American Society of Civil Engineers. In 1937, with the rank of captain, Harwood took an early retirement from the Army, which — to ease the glut of junior officers in its ranks — had put together packages allowing officers to retain small pensions.

MARRIAGE — AND A BUILDING BOUGHT BY THE GROWING INSTITUTE

HARWOOD AND HIS FIRST wife, Harriet, had divorced in the late 1920s. Their life in Hawaii, where he was based at Schofield Army Barracks, had not suited her, and she had taken their three children and returned to the mainland. Harwood's bachelor years eventually were to come to an end, though. As he pursued his work with AIER, he was aided in doing so by his faithful employee, Helen Fowle — a strong-willed woman, five years his junior, who possessed a fiery disposition capable of matching wits and action with the energetic Harwood. Helen, middle name of Longfellow, came from old New England stock. She'd overcome childhood polio and as a young woman daringly bridged the gender gap by working as a sports reporter for the *Boston Globe*.

> "During the 1920s, E.C. Harwood published his findings concerning the then ominous business-cycle implications of unsound credit creation, and it was the accuracy of his findings that facilitated AIER's founding in 1933. Over the years, we have revised and expanded our efforts to monitor current business-cycle developments, and analyses of money and credit trends remain an important part of our research."
>
> — *AIER After 70 Years: Our History and Plans for the Future*

In 1938, Edward and Helen married. The Institute was proving to be a going concern — now with 50 employees, mostly performing clerical work — and more workspace was needed. As Helen later wrote, "In our after-dinner strolls around Cambridge we discovered a boarded-up, three-story former fraternity house on Dunster Street, a block-and-half from Harvard Square." The Georgian-style brick building near Harvard's main gate was in sad disrepair. A snowstorm had deposited three feet of snow through an open skylight. Harwood shrewdly negotiated with the bank that held the mortgage. The house, he pointed out, was a nonperforming loan with a leaking roof. He was offering to take it off the bank's bad-loan books. And that's how AIER bought the building at 54 Dunster St. for $30,000, securing a 30-year mortgage at 3 percent.

AIER's staffers pitched in to remodel the warped floors, broken windows and peeling walls. Harwood recruited his two brothers, Harry and Bill, and the three set to work rehabilitating the building. The results were office space on the ground floor, staff apartments on the upper two floors, and a basement apartment for a caretaker. It is easily imaginable that Harvard officials would have been chagrined — after seeing the once dilapidated building restored to functional use — at having let such a prime property a stone's throw from the campus' front gate be bought by someone else. (Harvard would literally pay the price for this oversight a half-dozen years hence.)

AIER began operations in its new headquarters in summer 1939. Now owning property in its own name, it incorporated. The Institute could boast of several hundred annual sustaining members, several hundred additional subscribers to the *Research Reports* and the *Investment Bulletin*, and 100,000 people who'd bought at least one of AIER's publications.

Neither Mr. nor Mrs. Harwood could have foreseen how the Institute would grow and grow — although its progress, along with that of countless institutions of American life — would be temporarily impeded by a world war. ❖

A PUBLISHED AUTHOR AT 33

Lt. E.C. Harwood — in 1931, serving as associate professor of military science and training at the Massachusetts Institute of Technology.

When Edward C. Harwood published *Cause and Control of the Business Cycle*, in 1932, it earned favorable mention by the Book-of-the-Month Club. Some readers may have regarded his background as odd for that of an economist — he was then a first lieutenant in the U.S. Army and an associate professor in military science at the Massachusetts Institute of Technology. But his book was based upon his analytical works that had led him to pen more than 100 published magazine, journal and newspaper articles to date.

Originally a self-taught economist who later added a master's of business administration degree, Harwood had studied government and banking excess for years, and had built himself a reputation for prediction — including that of the massive U.S. economic contraction that became known as the Great Depression. A series of his articles in *The Annalist* in 1928 and 1929 issued dire warnings.

Harwood's article, "The Probable Consequences to Our Credit Structure of Continued Gold Export," ran in March 1928, and noted that gold export would necessitate either a large reduction in bank reserves or — *if* the accepted 75 percent reserve requirement were maintained — a giant reduction in bank loans, because $1 billion of reserves supported "some $15.2 billion of deposits in member banks." He continued that because member and non-member Federal Reserve banks were fully extended, and Reserve banks themselves could not export gold without a drastic drop in deposits, the nation's credit "shoe" was likely to pinch.

The next month, *The Annalist* ran another Harwood article, "The Underlying Causes of Our Recent Prosperity: Why the End Is Near." Harwood opined that, "Business has already started on the downward part of the [business] cycle." In February 1929, his article, "Speculation in Securities vs. Commodity Speculation," asserted, "It is plain, therefore, that the future holds undesirable possibilities. There is every indication that the lesson as to liquidity of loans on securities will be forcibly impressed on bankers and business men in the not far distant future."

Harwood's sounding of an alarm was repeated in his article in August 1929, titled, "Deterioration of the American Bank Portfolio — a Ratio Analysis, 1920-28." He concluded: "It seems to this writer that the concrete evidence herein presented offers a far more satisfying explanation of the prosperity of the past few years than the 'new-era' brand of reasoning; and further, that the time may not be far distant when the country will realize, in the light of a cold gray 'morning after,' that it has just been on another credit-splurging spree."

Two months later, the reality of that "credit-splurging spree" hit home on Oct. 28 — "Black Monday" — when the Dow Jones Industrial Average plummeted 13 percent, to be followed by another 12 percent drop the following day, with no ensuing rally. By 1931, about $50 billion (or approximately $500 billion in today's dollars) had been lost to investors in the stock market alone.

Cause and Control of the Business Cycle would end up being the first of nine books Harwood would publish in his lifetime. The others: *What Will Devaluation Mean To You?*, 1934; *Life Insurance from the Buyer's Point of View*, 1935; *Current Economic Delusions*, 1938; *Reconstruction of Economics*, 1955; *Useful Economics*, 1956; *Twentieth-Century Common Sense*, 1958; *Useful Procedures of Inquiry*, 1973; *A Current Appraisal of the Behavioral Sciences*, 1973.

BEHIND EVERY GREAT MAN, A GREAT WOMAN

On Sept. 7, 1937, E.C. Harwood, director of the American Institute for Economic Research, sent the following letter to his secretary, Helen Longfellow Fowle:

Dear Miss Fowle:

In accordance with the terms of the AGREEMENT AND DECLARATION OF TRUST OF THE AMERICAN INSTITUTE FOR ECONOMIC RESEARCH, you are hereby formally appointed a member of the Faculty of this organization. This will confirm the informal arrangements which have been in effect for several months past.

This appointment is made in recognition of your professional attainments and unremitting zeal in furthering the welfare of the organization as a whole, as well as your own part of the work. I believe that American Institute for Economic Research, and through it the American public, will be well served by the professional ability and devotion to duty which have characterized your efforts in the past.

The following year, Harwood and Fowle consummated a different, more permanent, relationship. They married on Oct. 29, 1938, and went on to have four children: two sons and two daughters. Together, Edward and Helen would steward AIER for the better part of four decades. Each was intellectual, individualistic, energetic and prolific. Helen, for example, had forged a career as a newspaper reporter in an era long before women professionals were commonplace in the American workforce, let alone the rough-and-tumble jungle of a newspaper sports department.

Many years later, Helen recalled her departure from a promising career in an essay she titled, "Almost":

Helen Longfellow Fowle — who would add the surname Harwood in 1938.

It was the depth of the Depression, and I was no longer starry-eyed about working on a newspaper. From being glamorous, it had become just a job like almost any other. When an interesting offer of a position with shorter hours and more pay as an editorial assistant came along, I accepted it.

Word got around. The Boston Globe's *Sunday editor Larry Winthrop, for whom I had done some pieces, called me into his office to ask if I knew what I was doing. Was I, a good reporter, really throwing over a newspaper job to sit in a stuffy office up on Beacon Hill and edit economic foolishness from 9 to 5? Much pleased and genuinely surprised by his concern I wavered, then almost called Dr. Godfrey to tell him that his Engineering-Economics Foundation would have to get along without me; journalism needed me more. Almost . . . but the prospect of more regular income (at* The Globe *I was on "space," which paid 28 cents for each inch of published copy, as I remember) plus not having to stumble down Newspaper Row late at night to file a story for the morning edition and then rush to catch the last train home, won out. Just barely.*

The non-profit Foundation depended on private donations to exist. Predictably in that Depression time it soon ran out of funds and I joined the ranks of the unemployed. However, I had savings and lived at home, and at first snootily turned down the few job openings that came my way, expecting that surely God's gift to the writing profession would be offered something challenging before long.

Nothing was. I thought about asking for my old position on The Globe *back, but the girl who had replaced me was doing a good job, and I knew that most of my fellow reporters in the Sports section had families and were probably having a hard time of it. No editor with any compassion would fire one of them to take back even as gifted an individual as I.*

Then one night during routine perusal of the Boston Transcript's *scanty little Help Wanted column an item caught my eye. Someone at MIT needed an editorial assistant to help prepare manuscripts "and perform other routine duties." Oh, Lord! — probably another camouflaged ad for a typist! I almost didn't clip it out, but there was nothing else even slightly in my line or*

CHAPTER 1

for which I felt at all qualified. And the bottom of my savings account was in sight.

An MIT professor who lived next door in Winchester might know something about that job. I trotted over. "Oh, that guy," he said. "I don't know . . . he's in the military science department, but he talks occasionally to economics classes." Having gone down with one economics enterprise, the prospect of tying up with another didn't appeal, and I almost threw the clipping away.

However, the next withdrawal from a dwindling savings account indicated that I'd soon be a parasite on my father, who was struggling with shrinking income himself. So I called the number given in the ad. A mild-sounding male voice said the position was still open, and would pay the munificent sum of $12 a week. I almost hung up; the last job offer that I'd disdained paid $15. Yes, there would be some typing. In my previous job I'd had my own secretary to take over the typing chores; again I almost hung up. However, a flashback to that dwindling bank balance made me ask for an interview.

Several times in the intervening days I almost canceled the appointment. However, when the day came I borrowed my sister's most becoming hat, put on a tailored suit and white gloves, and showed up at MIT. The job had so little appeal that I didn't bother to be on time and knocked at the door of Room 114 slightly past the hour agreed upon. When that same controlled male voice answered, I turned the knob and found myself looking down into the very brown eyes of my future husband.

I typed for that man the rest of his life.

REVIEWS OF 'WHAT WILL DEVALUATION MEAN TO YOU?'

E.C. Harwood's 64-page booklet, *What Will Devaluation Mean to You?*, was the first publication by the American Institute for Economic Research, and garnered mention by the Book-of-the-Month Club and reviews in a smattering of newspapers and financial publications. Here is a sampling:

From *Modern Finance*, Sept. 1, 1936:

Under the caption, "Time to tell the truth" the author writes: "The forgotten man has been tried and found guilty of possessing something which can be taken from him. Surely he has the right to know what may prove to be the details of his sentence to economic death."

The American Institute for Economic Research is neither a political nor a commercial organization. It is entirely independent, and represents no fund or concentrated source of wealth.

Careful provisions insure that neither the Institute itself nor members of its staff shall derive profit from organizations or businesses which happen to be benefited by the results of research.

Chapter headings are self-explanatory. In addition to the title chapter, intriguing discussions follow on protection of income against rising cost of living; devaluation and your investments; adjusting life insurance plans to a smaller dollar.

* * *

From *Trust Companies*, a monthly financial publication, in April 1934:

This publication is made up of six articles, seven pages being devoted to the subject as indicated by the above title. The other five articles are entitled, Adjusting Life Insurance Plans to a Smaller Dollar; Preserving the Buying Power of Savings; What to Do with Future Savings; Protection Against a Rising Cost of Living; Devaluation and Your Investments.

The opening paragraphs preceding this series of articles read:

"If speculators and wealthy men in this country have not yet arranged their affairs so as to profit enormously by the devaluation process, they have only themselves to blame. For months past, the expensive advisory services, individual investment advisors, and professional economists have been telling their clients how to protect themselves and reap huge rewards as a consequence of present monetary policies. It has been reported that one of the Administration's monetary 'experts' recently admitted to a Senate committee that devaluation '. . . would give to the well informed almost complete assurance of early uncontrollable credit expansion. . . .'

"It does not seem to occur to those guiding Administration policies, nor to their ardent supporters in the pulpit and elsewhere, that the billions piled upon billions shortly to be delivered to vested interests, concentrated wealth, and the speculator class will necessarily be at the expense of the Forgotten Man. A rising cost of living will automatically reduce his share of goods produced.

"This, however, is not an attempt to stop the process. Nor is it a criticism, either of those at present in power or their policies. It is merely an effort to state in simple language the unbiased truth about the results to be expected. The Forgotten Man has been tried and found guilty of possessing something which can be taken from him. Surely he has the right to know what may prove to be the details of his sentence to economic death."

The following definite predictions made by Professor Harwood in articles published in leading financial and economic journals during the past five years are cited in advance of the first article:

- *That the time may not be far distant when the country will realize, in the light of a cold gray 'morning after,' that it has just been on another credit-splurging spree. August 1929. (Stocks started downward the next month.)*
- *That business was not fundamentally sound and that banks would fall in "wholesale lots." November 1929.*
- *That stimulation of new construction would not only fail to cure but would tend "to prolong the current depression." May 1930.*

- *That the climax of liquidation and the low for high-grade bonds would occur "about the end of May" 1932. April 1932. (The low for bonds was May 31, 1932.)*
- *That "Technocracy" was just another fad of the moment without either logical background or help for the future. December 1932. ("Technocracy" is almost forgotten, now.)*
- *That serious discussion of a planned inflation or devaluation in legislative halls would lead to runs on banks, and the "banking system would collapse like a house of cards." January 1933. (Two months later the collapse came.)*

* * *

From the *Columbus Citizen*, July 28, 1934:

Inflation effects on the common man and how he can protect his savings and investments against further devaluation of the dollar, are explained in a new book by E.C. Harwood.

This book is published by the American Institute for Economic Research, Cambridge, Mass., a non-political and a non-commercial organization.

The articles are titled, "What Will Devaluation Mean to You," "Adjusting Life Insurance Plans to a Smaller Dollar," "Preserving the Buying Power of Savings," "What To Do with Future Savings," "Protection Against a Rising Cost of Living," "Devaluation and Your Investments."

The material is written in a straightforward manner with the ideas presented clearly and concisely. Many new thoughts never before published should cause this book to receive widespread distribution.

* * *

John D. Van Becker, financial editor of the *San Francisco Call-Bulletin* newspaper, devoted an entire column in the April 2, 1934, issue, to E.C. Harwood's theories on devaluation:

Regardless of its general effects in the scaling down of the debt level, devaluation forces this inescapable conclusion: the forgotten man is being "taken for a ride," declares E.C. Harwood, a member of the faculty of the Massachusetts Institute of Technology. His recent book on "Cause and Control of the Business Cycle" attracted wide attention in that he attributed the boom of 1929 and the subsequent depression to an orgy of excessive bank credit and an unwarranted increase in purchasing power.

Professor Harwood, trustee for the American Institute of Economic Research of Cambridge, has written a series of five bulletins on how the forgotten man, in a measure, may protect himself from the effects of devaluation. He covers: adjusting life insurance plans, preserving the buying power of savings, what to do with future savings, protection against a rising cost of living, and devaluation and investments.

The ride, engineered by devaluation and on which the forgotten man is embarked, is the continuing pressure of the high cost of living. Devaluation or clipping the coinage, as the process was called in the days of the robber kings, is just a subtle form of taxation, the economist declares. Like most other taxes, he points out, those imposed by this insidious method must be borne by the forgotten man.

Prices are rising, but there is some doubt as to the rate of this advance, Professor Harwood asserts. This is because the extent of such forces as credit expansion cannot at this time be ascertained. But if the price level is determined by the mere result of devaluation so far, we arrive at a value of 150 as the index number or per cent that prices will be in terms of pre-war levels. This is 5 per cent higher than the price level which existed during 1926. The economist significantly adds:

It is important to realize that this computation of the price level to be expected gives the minimum and not the maximum. The 150 per cent level is the result to be expected even though the slowest means by which devaluation can achieve its results is adhered to.

The minimum, however, may exist only as a hope for the forgotten man, the economist infers. For he is face to face with the possibility of higher costs of living than in 1930. In view of the fact that the cost-of-living index was still as high as 127, in 1932, he says, it is not unreasonable to suppose that when the effects of the devaluation process have been fully realized the cost of living will be 212 as compared to the pre-war level of 100. This is even higher than the peak year of 1920.

It may be considered fairly certain, Professor Harwood goes on, that the cost of living within the next few years will move above the 200 per cent level. It certainly is not unreasonable to assert, he adds, that prices may become as high as they were in 1929. Then he fires this double-barrel:

The devaluation process has been tried before. "Controlled" inflation as a means of bootstrap lifting has a long and unsavory record. In general, it is safe to say that no nation has ever abandoned such methods until a majority of the people realized the hopeless futility of the process.

There will be a period of prosperity while the devaluation mechanism is working out its effects. But serious maladjustments will inevitably arise exactly similar in principle to those which made necessary the collapse in 1929 and the present depression.

THE 1940S:

AFTER WAR'S INTERRUPTION, AIER FINDS A PERFECT CAMPUS

B y 1940, the U.S. economy was on the upswing, and the consensus among economists was that the Great Depression was over. Lawmakers critical of the New Deal's cost and the growth of federal power were succeeding in dismantling many of the alphabet programs. But the shrinking of government would prove to be very short-lived.

After the Japanese Navy's surprise attack on the U.S. Naval base at Pearl Harbor, Hawaii, on Dec. 7, 1941, the United States soon found itself fighting a large-scale war in the Pacific against the Empire of Japan, and in North Africa and Europe against the Axis Powers of Germany and Italy. From then until Japan's final surrender on Aug. 15, 1945, federal spending would come to total $321 billion — about twice as much as all U.S. government spending, combined, from the first federal budget in 1789.

This was the period of G.I. Joe and Rosie the Riveter; of war bonds and victory gardens. The U.S. government during World War II became the leading sector of the nation's economy, funding the mobilization and arming of 12 million drafted soldiers and a full-scale war effort that included controls on consumer prices and raw materials, bans on new housing and automobiles, rationing and subsidized wages, war production and bond campaigns. Six million women took temporary jobs in production and manufacturing to sustain

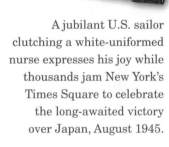

A jubilant U.S. sailor clutching a white-uniformed nurse expresses his joy while thousands jam New York's Times Square to celebrate the long-awaited victory over Japan, August 1945.

President Harry S Truman (1884-1972) at a press conference. He signed the Marshall Plan.

July 1944: English economist John Maynard Keynes (center) attends the United Nations International Monetary and Financial Conference, at the Mount Washington Hotel, in New Hampshire.

the war machinery.

In July 1944, as the Allies' victory seemed assured, 730 delegates from 44 Allied countries met at the Mount Washington Hotel in Bretton Woods, New Hampshire, to rebuild the international economic system by establishing rules for financial and commercial relations among the major independent

industrialized nations. The system of monetary management that was negotiated paved the way for the World Bank and the International Monetary Fund, and obligated each nation to adopt a monetary policy that tied the nation's currency-exchange rate within a fixed value of plus or minus 1 percent in terms of gold (and the IMF's ability to correct temporary imbalances of payments).

The war's end ushered in an extended economic boom in America that would last two decades. Americans built houses, bought new cars, and sustained a population growth known as the Baby Boom. In 1948, President Harry S Truman signed the Marshall Plan to reconstruct devastated Europe, and the United States contributed more than $13 billion in economic and technical aid, which further boosted the U.S. economy as European nations bought U.S. products. By 1949, Wall Street began an uninterrupted bull run that would last eight years. Characteristic of consumer confidence, a third-party credit card — the Diners'

Nuclear bomb test, Nevada Test Site.

Club — was established, and ordinary Americans began carrying the cards in their wallets.

HARWOOD HEEDS WAR'S CALL; AIER STRUGGLES ALONG

AMERICA'S ENTRANCE INTO THE war had an immediate effect on AIER. Sales of publications fell, sustaining memberships declined, and faculty members left for military service. By late 1941, only four faculty remained on a full-time basis, and the clerical force decreased to a third of its strength.

Ever the patriot, E.C. Harwood answered the call to duty by ending his retirement from the Army and leaving AIER in the capable hands of wife Helen. Even with Harwood soon serving abroad — shipped to England to help plan the invasion of Normandy, then (after promotion to colonel) transferred to Leyte, the Philippines, with Gen. Pat Casey to prepare for Gen. Douglas MacArthur's triumphant return to those islands — the Institute never missed printing an issue of its then weekly *Research Reports*. What made the difference between AIER's survival and death was the $10,000 or so in annual income from the 300 or so annual sustaining members who continued their support during the war years.

The fierce daily bombing and strafing from the Japanese air force on Leyte eventually took a psychological toll on Col. Harwood, who was handling the work of a brigadier general who'd been wounded. In April 1945, Col. Harwood was given a medical discharge. His stalwart service in two war theaters had earned him the Legion of Merit and the Bronze Star. His time abroad also yielded him two discoveries that would enormously serve the mission of AIER after his return. The first discovery came while he was momentarily idled in New Guinea. Voraciously reading journals, he came upon the cooperative work, by American philosophers John Dewey and Arthur Bentley, on a scientific method for the social sciences, which would become known as the "transactional approach" to problem solving, and serve as the basis for their landmark book in 1949, *Knowing and the Known*. Their approach to acquiring useful knowledge would form a core aspect of AIER's scientific methodology. Breaking from philosophical and scientific systems of the past, the transactional approach uses inquiry in which the observer accepts existing descriptions of events only on a tentative and preliminary basis, and allows for new descriptions of the phases and aspects of events, based on inquiry, to be made at any time. Therefore, use of the approach avoids semantic traps that can hinder clear, objective observation and analysis. The observer enjoys the right to investigate any subject matter in any manner that seems appropriate, under reasonable hypothesis. There are no hard, immutable truths that can never be challenged. Everything is left open to questioning and testing, the results scrupulously assessed. The method precludes making absolute predictions of events; the observer can only say that, based on warrants, what events may occur.

The second great discovery Col. Harwood made in New Guinea was reading a real-estate catalogue, which featured an item on an abandoned estate in western Massachusetts. This particular estate, Edgewood, was in the Berkshire Hills, in the town of Great Barrington, not far from the New York state line. Of the 500 acres, the advertising listing said, 85 percent was fine timber and the remainder open meadowland. A small lake, called Long Pond, and a trout stream were on the property, as well as 12 miles of bridle paths, a 100-tree apple orchard, and a three-story stone English manor house built in 1929, complete with servant quarters and pantries, elevator, large laundry and four-car garage. There also were a nine-room guest cottage and other outbuildings, a farm barn and sheep barn, cow stable and dairy house. The estate's owner held the mortgage free and clear. Edgewood seemed a candidate as a site on which to relocate AIER in a permanent home.

THE COLONEL RETURNS; AIER FINDS A NEW HOME AND RENEWED SPIRIT

AFTER COL. HARWOOD WAS invalided home from the Philippines, he and wife Helen purchased the 103-acre core of Edgewood from its owner, a local lumberman named Lawrence Barbieri, who had acquired the estate a year earlier. The deflated price: $25,000. Sale of the brick house on Dunster Street in Cambridge fetched nearly twice that sum — making the property in Great Barrington an easy deal to swing. The secluded estate, with its stone manor situated at the end of a winding, mile-long road, included a large stone house, outbuildings, a pristine water supply and

stunning views of the rolling Berkshire Hills and majestic Taconic Range.

The following year, Col. Harwood retired from the Army a second time and set to work preparing AIER's new headquarters. In the weekly *Research Reports* issue of Aug. 4, 1946, Col. Harwood announced:

"To Annual Sustaining Members and Subscribers:

"By the time you are reading this, the Institute will be operating in its new home at Great Barrington, Massachusetts. This is in the Berkshire Hills and has direct rail and parkway connections to New York City.

"Although the former quarters in Cambridge, Massachusetts, offered some advantages, the Institute was outgrowing its limited space and other facilities. Furthermore, better living and working conditions for the staff were needed.

"A research organization must not retreat to an ivory tower, far removed from contact with the economic realities of life. Such conditions discourage the frequent testing of theories against experience, without which research tends to become sterile, as John Dewey has often emphasized.

"Fortunately, the economic realities of life are found in the country as well as in the cities. It may well be that those who live in the country have an advantage, because the economic processes are less hidden by the complexity of modern life. Furthermore, in the larger financial centers, there is often a preoccupation with immediate developments that lessens perspective. Those who would think effectively must stand aside from the flood current of multitudinous minutiae

> "In effect, you are saying that there are available in the hands of the public large quantities of unused purchasing power or stagnant or partially used purchasing power which the Government can obtain. In that, I believe you are mistaken. In fact, I have already been at some pains to analyze that aspect of the problem and have proved, by logic and facts, that your supposition is erroneous.
>
> "Therefore, I assert without qualification that you are recommending a policy of inflation, and that the Administration is following such a policy. . . . The inevitable result will be another collapse, the severity of which will be dependent upon the degree of inflation reached."
>
> — *E.C. Harwood, in a letter of Feb. 8, 1934, to John Maynard Keynes*

that clutter our daily affairs.

"The choice of a site for the Institute's permanent home had been under consideration for several years. The Asheville, North Carolina, Colorado Springs, San Diego, San Francisco, and other areas had all been investigated; but the desirability of being near to the principal financial center of the world was an important factor in the final decision. Furthermore, it now appears probable that the future capital of the world, if UN does so develop, will also be conveniently accessible.

"Surprising as it may seem, our new home was tentatively selected by me while in New Guinea two years ago. From many listed in a previews catalogue, seven estates in the Berkshire area were chosen, and this was the one that seemed best suited to the Institute's needs. Shortly after my return from the Philippines last year, arrangements were made to acquire the property, and it was prepared for the Institute's occupancy during the winter and spring of this year.

"The principal building is a 31-room stone mansion, built in 1929-1931 but not quite completed and never before occupied. The story of this building and of the development of the estate by its first owner is interesting but is too long to include here. The building is ideally suited to the Institute's needs, and ample room for future development is available on the 100-acre estate.

"A map indicating the location of the new home is enclosed with this issue of the bulletin. You are cordially invited to visit the Institute whenever convenient. Accommodations for members and other guests are available by advance arrangement.

"It is our hope and belief that the favorable living and working conditions will prove stimulating. As our research progresses, after the stagnant period of the war years, we look forward to an increasing ability to aid in preserving the best that has been inherited from the past, and assist in building wisely for the future."

BUCOLIC AREA, STEEPED IN HISTORY, DREW DREAMERS BEFORE AIER'S ARRIVAL

The rustic, remote region of southwestern Massachusetts where the American Institute for Economic Research set up its permanent home in 1946 is steeped in history. The wooded beauty of the estate itself — set within the town limits of Great Barrington, between the rolling Berkshire Hills and the Taconic Range —beckoned visions of dreamers before the Institute set up its campus there.

Frederick Stark Pearson, world-renowned engineer, built this wooden manor on a knoll on his vast estate he called Edgewood. A subsequent owner, Prentice Coonley, razed the house and built in its place a great stone house he called Cotswold.

First, the history. In early Colonial times, New York and Massachusetts each claimed the area, which retained a wild character and beckoned, as one historian noted, "enclaves of entrepreneurs," adding, "those entrepreneurs were known to be mostly horse thieves and tax evaders in hiding." In the same period, a Connecticut goldsmith named "Mr. Belcher" counterfeited King George's currency in a limestone cave next to Main Street in Great Barrington, where Belcher's Square stands at the intersection of routes 7 and 23.

In the nearby town of Egremont stands a limestone monument to Shays Rebellion. Daniel Shays, who served as a captain in the Continental Army during the Revolution, led small farmers in a popular insurrection in 1786 in protest of crushing debt and stiff state taxes on land, polls, and whiskey, as well as a depressed local economy, judicial abuses and outrageous rents paid to absentee landlords, including speculators from eastern Massachusetts. A Massachusetts militia repelled an attack by the Shaysites on the federal armory in Springfield, but the lack of an institutional response — and the spread of propaganda labeling the Shaysites as anarchists — led attendees at the 1787 Constitutional Convention in Philadelphia to strengthen the role of central government.

A century later, Great Barrington earned a different footnote in history, becoming the first town in the world with alternating-current streetlights. William Stanley, chief engineer for George Westinghouse in Pittsburgh, moved to Great Barrington, where in 1886 he demon-

CHAPTER 2

strated his new electric power transformer by illuminating offices and stores on Main Street with an AC electric generator powered by water turbines on the Housatonic River. Within a few years, the many riverside mills in this area adopted economical AC electricity and replaced dangerous mechanical belt drives with electric generators and motors.

A FAMOUS ENGINEER, AND A STOCK SPECULATOR, TRY TO CREATE PARADISE

NOW, FOR THE DREAMERS.

In 1902, Frederick Stark Pearson, a world-renowned hydroelectric and industrial engineer who'd become a millionaire before age 30, attended a conference of the American Institute of Electrical Engineers in Great Barrington. Smitten by the area, he began acquiring land of the old Tuller Farm on Seekonk Crossroads, which became the nucleus for an estate that spread to 13,000 acres. On the knoll where AIER's stone manor now stands, Pearson built a large, wooden, Victorian-style house. He had man-made ponds, including Long Pond, built, fashioned a two-acre terraced garden and imported rare shrubbery, rhododendrons and other plants from countries with similar climes. He added a five-mile road leading from the manor to the top of Tom Ball Mountain and had workmen cut miles of woodland drives and bridal paths through the rough forests and former hayfields. He stocked the grounds with imported Guernsey cattle and grouse, rare pheasants from Hindustan and deer and peccaries from Mexico. His extensive game preserve featured a 7-foot-tall, seven-mile-long fence to keep his deer from escaping. He supported his estate — named "Edgewood" — with a working farm that included prize-winning sheep.

Pearson also maintained residences in New York City and Surrey, England. Only a few years after completing his modest house at Edgewood, Pearson and his wife, Mabel, tragically perished on the *RMS Lusitania* steamship luxury liner, torpedoed by a German submarine off the Irish coast in May 7, 1915. Eleven years later, a Chicago stockbroker,

Frederick Stark Pearson, 1910. His Edgewood estate came to comprise about 13,000 acres.

Frederick Stark Pearson with his family at Edgewood.

Prentice Coonley, who'd married the Crane Plumbing heiress, purchased the 500-acre heart of the estate. Coonley razed the manor house and began construction of a 31-room stone house, christened Cotswold, and meant to copy the style of the large limestone houses in the Cotswold Hills north of Bath, England. While those houses are made from the local limestone, little of it was imported for Coonley's Cotswold; instead, stone for the thick walls was quarried from Mount Hunger in Monterey, Massachusetts.

Coonley never completed his dream mansion. It was 90 percent finished by the time he lost his fortune — due to investment speculation — in 1932. He and his wife and their two daughters never got to live in the house, which they named "Folly Farm."

THE HARWOODS PICK UP A DREAM ESTATE AT A BARGAIN RATE

A LOCAL LUMBERMAN NAMED Lawrence Barbieri had acquired 500 acres of the property by 1944, drawn by the stands of pine and mixed hardwoods. As Col. Harwood and wife Helen searched during the World War II years for a suitable new, permanent campus for AIER, they considered the abandoned estates in southwestern Massachusetts. One particularly white elephant drew their attention: Edgewood, in the Berkshire Hills of southwestern Massachusetts. In 1945, for the bargain price of $25,000, they bought the core of "Folly Farm" — 103 acres, outbuildings, a water supply, and the nearly finished stone house. They sold AIER's property in Cambridge — the three-story brick house that Harvard University had passed on in the 1930s — for a tidy profit, and with the Institute's small staff began the work to put the new headquarters and campus for AIER into working order.

Here and there in the stone manor were reminders of Prentice Coonley's grand plans. The largest room in Cotswold was intended as a music room to house Pearson's 50-stop Aeolian organ — a scheme that faded with his wealth. Nevertheless, the bath that would have been his wife's sported matching pink marble toilet, basin and tub; and the pink bath that would have been his own featured Venetian marble and gold-plated fixtures. Hot and cold water basins were in each bedroom in the intended servants quarters, and private baths awaited the live-in cook, butler, and housekeeper. All of these rooms had sat empty, never occupied,

Frederick Stark Pearson with one of his prize-winning rams, 1912.

and the interior trim and some of the wooden floors had never been installed.

The good news was that the house had remained dry and intact, if dusty and unfinished. Water valves were opened, electric mains were closed, and the place was inhabitable. The grounds, neglected since the days the Pearsons had lived there, were another story. Nature had steadily encroached on the development. Frost had tumbled marble fountains and cracked the goldfish pond and the marble benches under rusting grape arbors. Brushy fields had defeated the Pearsons' formal gardens. Laurels and saplings had overrun the riding trails. Local hunters preyed on the imported exotic game. Twenty-foot-tall trees occupied the wide courtyard and blocked the gravel roads. Mounds of excavated dirt and building debris surrounded the unfinished stone manor. "Folly Farm," indeed.

But under the direction of Col. Harwood, AIER's staff began clearing away the refuse and rubble, painting walls and woodwork and finishing floors. Within a few months, the Harwood family had settled into the stone house, now proudly called Cotswold, and AIER was operating at its new headquarters, with lots of room for expansion in the years and decades to come. They came to call the great stone house "the Castle" — a name which informally stuck from then on.

Finally, a lasting dream was taking shape on the estate.

KEYNES VS. HARWOOD — JOUSTING WITH PENS

In early 1934, while an associate professor in military science at the Massachusetts Institute of Technology, and director of his newly formed American Institute for Economic Research, Edward Harwood conducted a dialogue via personal correspondence and the news media with world-renowned British economist John Maynard Keynes about Keynes' proposal to employ supposedly hoarded money as part of a cure for the Depression. Keynesian economics — advocating interventionist governmental action to stimulate an economy during a downturn — was wielding significant influence on economic and political theory, and carried clout in shaping governmental policy, including in the United States.

Keynes held that aggregate demand for goods, not improvement of potential output, was the key factor driving an economy, especially during a contraction. He argued that governments could promote consumer demand — provide an "inducement to invest" — at the macro level to fight deflation and high unemployment through a combination of two policies: reducing interest rates; and investing in infrastructure as a stimulus to a cycle of more production, citizen investment and spending.

Harwood, in comparison to Keynes, labored in relative obscurity, although he was enjoying rising stature among some economists as a formidable analyst of monetary-policy matters, a forecaster of economic trends. Harwood had penned a constant stream of financial articles published in journals and newspapers, and predicted the drastic downturn that deflated the speculative stock-market bubble of the Roaring Twenties and resulted in the Great Depression. In 1932, Harwood had published his first book, *Cause and Control of the Business Cycle*. In stark contrast to Keynes, Harwood averred that unsound banking practices created nominal aggregate demand that led to booms inevitably followed by busts. He'd developed a business-cycle theory, and an "Index of Inflating" to measure banking excesses.

Excepts from their exchanges:

Keynes, in an open letter to President Franklin D. Roosevelt on Dec. 31, 1933, wrote: "Thus, as the prime mover in the first stage of the technique of recovery, I lay overwhelming emphasis on the increase of national purchasing power resulting from Governmental expenditure which is financed by loans and is not merely a transfer through taxation, from existing incomes. Nothing else counts in comparison with this.

"In a boom, inflation can be caused by allowing unlimited credit to support the excited enthusiasm of business speculators. But in a slump Governmental loan expenditure is the only sure means of obtaining quickly a rising output at rising prices . . ."

Harwood, in an article published in North American Newspaper Alliance publications on Jan. 6, 1934: "No doubt you will agree that when a Government obtains purchasing power by issuing bonds and selling them to the public, the funds involved may come from either of two sources:

"1. That portion of current incomes the receivers thereof desire to save and invest, rather than spend for consumption goods.

"2. Credit originated by the banking system in the form of demand deposits subject to check . . . ordinarily made available to business for commercial purposes in order to represent newly produced goods and facilitate their distribution.

"It is clear that if funds be obtained for Government spending from the first source, the net result is merely to transfer purchasing power from existing incomes. If the one who chooses to save and invest placed his money in the savings bank instead of buying Government bonds, the purchasing power would probably be used by the bank to buy a first mortgage . . .

"Apparently you feel the purchasing power expended by the Government should come from the second source mentioned. That would involve origination of purchasing power by the banking system in precisely the same manner funds were created for the Government during the world war. In other words, you appear to favor inflation by the indirect route."

Keynes, in a letter to Harwood of Jan. 26, 1934: "The article which you contributed to the American press concerning my Open Letter to the President has just come into my hands. I am not sending any reply for publication. . . . the explanation of the divergence of our views is to be found . . . .where you argue that the funds involved have to come from one of two principal sources and imply that, if the money which the President spends on his programme is borrowed from the public, the effect will be to diminish by that amount the new developments financed by private industry. This, I am sure, is where we part company.

"The view you express is one which has been widely held by economists — indeed, I held it myself 10 years ago. I believe now, however, that it involves a fundamental fallacy which runs through most applications of the classical theory of political economy to practical affairs. The same assumptions which are required for this conclusion to hold will also prove that unemployment is impossible. The theory of a fixed loan fund, so to speak, is in my present belief a complete fallacy."

Harwood, in a letter to Keynes of Feb. 8, 1934, "It was very kind of you to take the trouble to write to me regarding our recent exchange of views via N.A.N.A. Of course, I have studied your 'Treatise on Money' . . . I have analyzed it sufficiently to ascertain what are believed to be the major fallacies.

"In the first place, my views do not logically exclude unemployment and other depression phenomena. Under separate cover, I am forwarding a copy of my book dealing with the situation in detail. Nor am I committed to any 'fixed loan fund' theory.

Keynes, in a letter of Jan. 26, 1934, wrote, "The expenditure under the President's programmes will increase incomes and the excess of these increased incomes over current expenditure on consumption of goods will necessarily be exactly equal to what the President is borrowing. It makes no difference whatever to this whether he borrows direct from the public or by an increase of credit originated by the banking system.

"I have made some tentative advances towards establishing this view in my Treatise on Money, but I hope to make it much clearer in my next publication."

Harwood, in a letter of Feb. 8, 1934, wrote: "In effect, you are saying that there are available in the hands of the public large quantities of unused purchasing power or stagnant or partially used purchasing power which the Government can obtain. In that, I believe you are mistaken. In fact, I have already been at some pains to analyze that aspect of the problem and have proved, by logic and facts, that your supposition is erroneous.

"Therefore, I assert without qualification that you are recommending a policy of inflation, and that the Administration is following such a policy. . . . The inevitable result will be another collapse, the severity of which will be dependent upon the degree of inflation reached, and the time involved (as well as other factors of less importance). . . . I fear that the process may not only becloud vital issues, but that the end may involve loss of much of civilization that seems to be worth preserving. (A list of definite predictions made in published articles during the past few years is enclosed.)"

THE TWO MEN ARGUED other points in their respective letters of Dec. 31, 1933 (from Keynes), and Jan. 6, 1934 (from Harwood). One point was on the quantity theory of money:

Keynes: "The other set of fallacies, of which I fear the influence, arises out of a crude economic doctrine commonly known as the quantity theory of money. Rising output and rising incomes will suffer a set-back sooner or later if the quantity of money is rigidly fixed. Some people seem to infer from this that output and income can be raised by increasing the quantity of money . . ."

Harwood: "It hardly seems reasonable to suppose that one who so regarded the 'crude economic doctrine commonly known as the quantity theory of money' would favor inflation. This is one very perplexing feature of your letter. Apparently you advocate increasing the amount of the purchasing medium in circulation, but you feel this does not necessarily raise output and income.

"The only alternative which occurs to me is that you believe there are stagnant pools of purchasing power which should be in use and which can be drained by selling Government bonds. The question is, where are these stagnant pools and can they actually be drained as you suggest?

"I can conceive of two possibilities you may have in mind. Perhaps you believe demand deposits are being hoarded; or perhaps you think hoarders of actual currency would be willing to buy Government bonds.

"Demand deposits are not being hoarded. The velocity of circulation compares favorably with that of normal periods of prosperity in the past, though less than during the 1929 boom, as might be expected. So far as we can tell (the figures are both comprehensive and accurate), there are no stagnant pools of purchasing power in the form of demand deposits. Time or savings deposits are merely the record of funds handed to the banking system for investment purposes. There is no stagnant pool of purchasing power in connection with these records of past events.

"We have tried to coax currency out of hiding by offering Government bonds of small denomination, without success. In any event, the loss of purchasing power occasioned by such hoardings has been more than made up by Federal Reserve purchases of Government bonds and the issue of Federal Reserve notes."

Another point on which the two economists argued was how to sustain long-term investment. "Keynes cited the Roosevelt Administration's "National Industrial Recovery Act."

Keynes: "Could not the energy and enthusiasm which launched the N.R.A. in its early days be put behind a campaign for accelerating capital expenditure?"

Harwood: " . . . the proper sources of funds for long-term investment are . . . current incomes. . . . savings thus invested do not cause a reduction of consumer buying power . . ."

Keynes, in a letter of Feb. 28, 1934, wrote, "Thank you for your further letter. I am afraid, however, that we must be content to differ. I fancy that the origin of our difference is to be found rather deep down in the analysis and in particular in the meanings we give to the essential terms."

HISTORY VALIDATES HARWOOD'S VIEWS

WRITER JAGDISH MEHRA, AUTHOR of the *Economic Education Bulletin, Keynes vs. Harwood – A Contribution to Current Debate*, published in November 1985, pointed out that the U.S. government in the latter half of 1935 and throughout 1936 increased expenditures $400 million per month, consistent with Keynes' recommendation. Harwood's Index of Inflating indicated a recovery by mid-1935. He wrote in July 1935, "It is now possible to decide what criterion to apply in judging the success of the recovery program. Clearly, recovery alone is not the only test. . . . The vital and only satisfactory criterion is whether or not the recovery which comes in the next few months and years is sound and lasting."

Harwood predicted in the AIER *Research Reports* of May 3, 1937: "It is our belief that further large sales of Government bonds by the Reporting Member Banks would indicate that a substantial retreat back along the road of inflation . . . and that a minor depression at least comparable to the cyclical downturn in 1923 and 1924 is immediately ahead."

The forecast contraction began in May 1937 and lasted 13 months.

'THE INVESTMENT COUNSELOR RACKET'

E.C. Harwood penned the following essay in 1932. The version below has been condensed by Fred Harwood.

'The Investment Counselor Racket'

Historians have yet to choose a pithy label for the previous decade, but if by chance they choose the "racketeering decade," professional investment counselors will have to come to terms with their contribution to the decade's dubious distinction. Born in the early stages of the late bull market, the investment counselor racket flourished in that easy-money era.

Investment counselors are a varied lot. At one end of the spectrum quacks offer their subtle secrets on fancy charts and with graphic forecasts for the next "big move." At the other extreme move dignified professionals with university degrees and an exploitable economist or two.

To be sure, some legitimate advisory services furnish statistical information, charge a reasonable fee, and offer their estimates of the situation for what they may be worth. Their claims are modest and they make no pretensions to anything more than their own records justify. But for the speculator who wants something for nothing, such services cannot satisfy the demand for "tipster sheets" furnishing daily and weekly incentives to do something in the market.

Even those who pretend to be able to satisfy the desires of such speculators can hardly be taken seriously. As a whole, they give the margin trader a lively run for his money, and society cares little that his losses become the booty of shrewd tipsters.

On the other hand, among professional investment counselors is a class deserving of careful attention. This one has no scruples in choosing its unwitting victims. Posing as professionals, they approach unwary widows, individual trustees, and small institutions, and for a fat fee betray their confidence by leading the unfortunate investor into speculations for elusive quick profits.

An example can be found in the firm of Skotchem, Stickem, and Quack. (This preposterous title conceals the identity of those whose activities are detailed below. The facts, however, are believed to portray a representative situation.) Although such firms seldom make their schemes public, details of their advice given a small life insurance association are available. Because the experience of this client has been no different from that of many others, a brief investigation of the work of Skotchem, Stickem, and Quack will show what is to be expected from their type of service.

Several features of the relationship between the firm and its unfortunate client are of interest. First, the fee collected by Skotchem, Stickem, and Quack approximates $8,000 annually, which is 1/2 of 1 percent of the entire fund. Had the association so desired, it could have placed the funds in the care of a corporate trustee. Based on the present income from the fund, the compensation of a corporate trustee would approximate $6,000. The trustee would not only select proper investments, it would also make them, relieving the association of those details. In addition, the corporate trustee would assume definite legal responsibility for care of the funds in accordance with the trust instrument, and would distribute current income according to instructions.

In contrast with those services, Skotchem, Stickem, and Quack assumed no responsibility whatsoever. All the details of making investments, caring for securities and collecting income therefrom remained with the association officials. The investment counselor furnished only advice while collecting a fee nearly 50 percent greater than the cost of employing a corporate trustee.

Second, as anyone who has ever invested funds is well aware, the extra half of 1 percent return is obtainable only by assuming more risk, or a choice between strictly high-grade bonds and those of lesser rating. Choosing that type of professional investment counsel burdens the investor with an initial handicap. In order to obtain the same return, the client must take a greater risk.

Apparently, Skotchem, Stickem, and Quack knew that the expense of their services could be justified only by larger net return. Presumably in order to provide that justification, they recommended that the small insurance association invest part of its funds in common stocks. At first thought, and since certain states authorize some common stock investments for life insurance funds, this may not seem at all peculiar. In order to appreciate the full significance of the recommendation, however, one must know something of the financial status of the association.

Starting many years ago on an assessment basis, this mutual benefit company later changed to a level premium legal reserve plan. In other words, like all the large insurance companies, it adopted a policy requiring the accumulation of reserves in accordance with American Experience Tables specifications. The process was somewhat slow, and by December 1928 the association had accumulated only 86 percent of its required reserves. It had no surplus, no capital, and lacked one-seventh of its full legal reserves. The situation called for the utmost conservatism in making investments because they had no contingency fund, surplus, or other sum available to offset investment losses.

In March 1929, the firm of Skotchem, Stickem, and Quack was called in as investment counselor. The firm prepared a report, which is noteworthy for its inadequacy, on the situation as they saw it. Leaving aside technicalities, the results obtained by numerous *fire* insurance companies were accepted as a guide to the investment policy of this *life* insurance association. The report showed a failure to comprehend the nature of the business and concluded that the chief weakness of the portfolio was the absence of common stocks. During the succeeding few months, Skotchem, Stickem, and Quack recommended the sale of many high-grade bonds in order to "invest" the proceeds in common stock. By December 1929, approximately one-quarter of the fund was in common stock purchased at or near the September highs of the long bull market.

The indulgent reader may feel that the recommendations made were simple errors such as anyone might make in judging the future. Unfortunately for Skotchem, Stickem, and Quack, this excuse is inappropriate. In December 1928, the chief economist in the firm spoke at an open meeting of a group of economists. He particularly warned them that investors purchasing stocks at that time "stood to lose anywhere up to 50 percent of their purchase price." Just three months later, despite that warning, he urged the Board of Directors of the small insurance association to adopt his firm's recommendations to *purchase stocks* at prices *well above* those existing in December 1928.

The results can be imagined by anyone familiar with the course of the stock market in the last three years. Practically all of the life insurance companies have survived the storm in splendid condition. None of them have defaulted mortgages and bonds that approach the amount of their capital and surplus. Although the bond market has been through a severe panic, the lowest quoted values do not indicate any danger for most insurance companies. (Required reserve is in most cases several times the sum of capital and surplus.) The unfortunate association guided by Skotchem, Stickem, and Quack, however, has no surplus and has now lost nearly 50 percent of its reserve fund. The serious situation had aroused some policyholders at the last annual meeting. In anticipation of questions from members, the Secretary-Treasurer wrote to Skotchem, Stickem, and Quack asking them to furnish a letter to be published in the Annual Report. This letter, dated Jan. 11, 1932, was written just two weeks after a member of the firm had spoken again before a group of economists. The letter defended the recommendations made by Skotchem, Stickem, and Quack and advised a continuation of the speculative policy.

That the firm of investment counselors was disposed to make allowances for its errors is unsurprising. However, the firm's economist just 14 days earlier had publicly stated "I further suggest that life insurance companies might be required to carry all investments in common stocks at 75 percent of their cost, amortized to 100 percent over a 10-year period. I believe that this would *dissuade* companies with an *inadequate surplus* from considering *common stocks*." Again a member of the firm said one thing in public before a group of economists and something quite different in private. Such paradoxical procedure is understandable. The firm seems to realize that only speculative profits can justify their fat fee, yet they wish the public to think they are conservative investment counselors. That unavoidable speculative risks are the consequence of the attempt to get speculative profits seems not to disturb these modern "con men."

The conditions shown in this specific example may well cause investors to think twice before entrusting the supervision of their funds to any counselor. Probably trustees handling small estates, widows having funds to invest, and others who cannot afford to take chances would be better off in the long run if they refused to pay more for advice than a corporate trustee would charge for taking entire responsibility. This is not to say that no honest and able investment counselors exist. However, whoever pays a fancy fee for investment advice will find such a fee justified only by the assumption of speculative risks. Judging from the record, the results seldom justify the risks assumed by investment counselors seeking fat fees.

CHAPTER THREE
THE 1950S:
POSTWAR EXPANSION AND COLD WAR POLITICS

TV time: Nuclear families gathered around the television set, a new household addition, in living rooms throughout America in the 1950s.

The postwar prosperity boom continued in the early 1950s, with the Dow Jones Industrial Average finally reaching — on Nov. 23, 1954 — its previous high established a quarter-century earlier, before the market crash that heralded the onset of the Great Depression. This was the era of cars laden with chrome, and black-and-white television sets proliferating in households; of Hula Hoops, and the crazy new sound of rock 'n' roll. However, the U.S. economy did fall into recession in 1953 and '54. The federal government's response was its now familiar contra-cyclical activism to tweak the economy, adopting as it had a growth model promulgated by the Council of Economic

Advisers, formed in 1946 to advise the U.S. president. The government reduced taxes, eased credit and increased public-works programs.

The council's approach helped establish Keynesianism — the policy of stimulating the economy during downturns by reducing interest rates and investing in infrastructure — as the nation's economic policy. A turning point had come in 1949. CEA chairman Edwin Nourse had declared that government spending came down to choosing between "guns and butter," but board member Leon Keyserling countered that a growing economy allowed big defense expenditures without sacrificing an improved standard

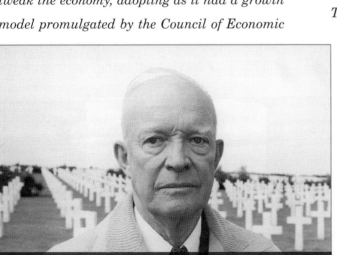

President Dwight D. Eisenhower stands before rows of white crosses at the St. Laurent Cemetery, France.

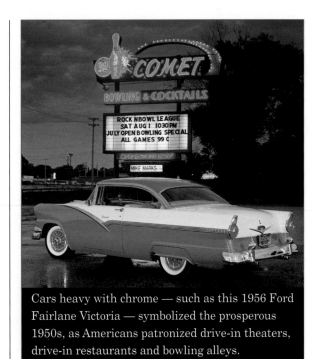

Cars heavy with chrome — such as this 1956 Ford Fairlane Victoria — symbolized the prosperous 1950s, as Americans patronized drive-in theaters, drive-in restaurants and bowling alleys.

space program absorbed ordinary Americans' thoughts. The U.S. military-industrial complex burgeoned, taking up an increasing share of the gross national product (and reaching 7 percent of GNP by the 1980s, at the peak of the arms race with the Soviet Union).

The economy continued to expand. By 1958, Americans could spend with three more universal credit cards, issued by Bank of America, American Express and Chase Manhattan.

AIER GROWS IN POSTWAR BOOM, WARNS OF STRUGGLE AT HOME

of living. Keyserling's view won out with the help of powerful presidential advisers; he replaced Nourse as chairman after Nourse resigned, sounding the alarm of the perils of "wasteful" defense costs and budget deficits.

A bloody military intervention on the Korean Peninsula from 1950-53 claimed nearly 34,000 U.S. combat deaths, as the Cold War with the Communist powers dominated the world political stage. Fears of atomic war and, toward the end of the decade, a battle for prestige in the

THE AMERICAN INSTITUTE FOR Economic Research continued to expand its operations. In 1957, the Institute added larger printing and mailing facilities just to the east of the Castle, connected by a convenient underground passageway. The Institute continued to present independent research on the economy — including the investment recommendation to buy common stocks. Conventional wisdom among economists was that the postwar economy would lapse into stagnation following the wind down from the

> 66From improved understanding of the behaviors of men in society we may reasonably hope for what men have sought since time began, not an Utopia of plenty and slothful ease but a civilization that will foster in every possible way the development of individual men to their maximum capacities and the firm establishment of a good society.99
>
> — Col. E.C. Harwood, from the article, "Scientific Breakthrough of the Twentieth Century," in the October 1957 issue of The American Journal of Economics and Sociology.

> **"**In saying that we believe the struggle against communism will be won, if it is won, here at home, we do not intend to belittle the sacrifices made by American men on Korean or other battlegrounds. What we do imply is that, no matter how many battles our men of the armed services win abroad, the long-term battle against communism may be lost here in the United States. Victory of the armed forces is probable, but preservation here at home of what they really have fought for is assured by no means.**"**
>
> — *Col. E.C. Harwood, "The Struggle Against Communism."*

war economy. But Col. Harwood saw that the glut of inflationary purchasing media and the pent-up consumer demand would create a prolonged postwar boom. (He was proved right.)

As for the Cold War itself, including the bloody conflict that raged on the Korean Peninsula in the first four years of the decade, Col. Harwood characteristically had his own view, which he spelled out in an essay titled, "The Struggle Against Communism":

"In saying that we believe the struggle against communism will be won, if it is won, here at home, we do not intend to belittle the sacrifices made by American men on Korean or other battlegrounds. What we do imply is that, no matter how many battles our men of the armed services win abroad, the long-term battle against communism may be lost here in the United States. Victory of the armed forces is probable, but preservation here at home of what they really have fought for is assured by no means.

"We think that they really have fought for progress toward the goals of the great revolution that began a few hundred years ago. This revolution has as its primary aims the security of life and liberty for individual men and the right to pursue happiness as they choose. We refer particularly to the individual's freedom to choose his goals, to equality of opportunity to earn, and to the right to have or to spend what one earns. We attribute the great material progress found in the United States primarily to the relatively greater freedom that has existed here in comparison with the situations in most other countries of the world.

"The struggle may be lost at home through a combination of complacency and confusion on the part of the general public and design on the part of those who would join the counterrevolutionary movement (socialism) in Western Civilization. For example, one of the most potent weapons of the counterrevolutionists elsewhere in the world has been inflation (Lenin stressed its importance, but he was neither the first nor the last to use it effectively). And inflation continues to rob the common man here in the United States." ❖

'ECONOMIC RESEARCH INSTITUTE IS BETTER KNOWN IN FAR CORNERS OF THE WORLD THAN IN BERKSHIRES'

The *Berkshire County Eagle* printed a lengthy, five-column feature story on the American Institute for Economic Research in the newspaper's issue of Nov. 26, 1952, under the headline above.

Here are excerpts:

GREAT BARRINGTON — It is a curious fact that the American Institute for Economic Research carries this town's name into the far corners of the world, but on its home grounds it is little spoken of. Accepted as a sort of Bartholomew's Cobble on the cultural landscape, it commands as much attention in Seattle as in Stockbridge, if not a bit more.

Yet there are things about the Institute, now in its 19th and most successful year, that are of interest anywhere. Few would guess, for example that:

Col. and Mrs. Harwood in 1957 with their children, from left: Katherine (front), Eve, William and Fred.

- It sells more booklets on economic subjects than any other research organization in the world.
- It has a gross income of $17,000 this month and more than $200,000 this year.
- It sends out well over 2,000,000 pieces of mail a year.
- Its publications help the average man avoid financial tangles, pick a good insurance policy and select the safest place to invest his small funds.
- It combines training and practical research in a full-fledged fellowship program.

OFFICER IN CHARGE

Carrying out all this activity is a staff of 25 headed by Col. Edward C. Harwood, a 52-year-old retired Army officer and authority on inflation and monetary policy. The publications and reports are prepared by an eight-member faculty, assisted this year by eight fellows, while other employees take care of the formidable secretarial, clerical and shipping duties.

The Institute's all-year job, which provides the basic income, is to put out two periodicals: the "Investment Bulletin," a bi-monthly guide for people with spare cash; and the "Research Reports," a weekly pamphlet on economic developments. About 1,500 "annual sustaining members," at $35 each, take the two services.

Over the past 18 years, these two periodicals have been the Institute's bread and butter, but now they supply only a quarter of the revenue. The other three-quarters comes from sale of the booklets written by staff members. They cover a wide range, as indicated by some of the titles: "How to Invest Wisely," "Where Will Tomorrow's Opportunities Be?" "Cause and Control of the Business Cycle," "How to Make Your Budget Balance," and "The Counterrevolution."

More than 100,000 of the booklets are sold each year, to a clientele that includes 30 U.S. senators and representatives and a number of colleges. Nearly 400,000 persons, 600 of them from Berkshire County, have bought at least one.

MILLIONAIRE'S MANSION

The 31-room building that houses the AIER was built in 1930 by Prentice L. Coonley, Chicago businessman and speculator, in a high woodland overlooking Long Pond on the Alford town line. It was never completed by the Coonleys, who lost most of their money, but the very simplicity and occasional lack of interior trim suit it for offices.

Most of the work is done in what was intended to be the music room. The organ loft at one side is now filled with book shelves; the rest of the room accommodates 17 desks, with quite a bit of space between them. Near at hand is a large room for the secretaries (with paneled walls and alabaster fireplace) and a suite for the voluminous filing and mailing work.

In one room is an automatic envelope-filling machine, perhaps the only one in the country, which can load as many as

An overhead view of the Institute's manor and surrounding grounds, 1955.

25,000 envelopes in a day. There are other huge rooms for other office machines and storage in the cellar, while elsewhere in the building are quarters for 18 persons, including the Harwoods and the fellows.

There are two dining rooms, which take care of from 15 to 18 at breakfast and dinner and 30 at lunch — and upstairs in the Harwoods' quarters is a really eye-popping bathtub. The pink marble monster was built by the Crane Company for the 1893 Exposition in Chicago, and Prentice Coonley is reputed to have taken it out of the company's Michigan Avenue show window for $3,500.

Col. Harwood gets a kick out of the bathtub, as well as the 18-inch-thick reinforced concrete and stone walls, the gold-plated bathroom fixtures, the "trunk room" (big as most living rooms) and the magnificent view from every angle of the house. But clearly he feels they are incidental to the Institute's mission.

"I'm convinced that in another quarter of a century, this will be a very important organization in the history of the country," he says. Without going into graphs and surveys and economic theory, you can be sure it has made a strong start.

'BREAKTHROUGH OF THE TWENTIETH CENTURY'

Col. Harwood's article, "Scientific Breakthrough of the Twentieth Century," appeared in the October 1957 issue of *The American Journal of Economics and Sociology*. Early in the article, Harwood cited John Dewey and Arthur F. Bentley's book, *Knowing and the Known*. An excerpt of Harwood's article:

In spite of 2,000 years of debate by the world's most eminent philosophers, including some of those living today, the question, What is 'knowledge'? has remained unanswered, or at best unsatisfactorily (inconsistently and incoherently) answered, until recent decades. The situation as it has been until these mid years of the twentieth century has been summarized in these words.

"Knowledge: In current employment this word is too wide and vague to be a *name* of anything in particular. The butterfly 'knows' how to mate, presumably without learning; the dog 'knows' its master through learning; man 'knows' through learning how to do an immense number of things in the way of arts and abilities; he also 'knows' physics, and 'knows' mathematics; he 'knows' *that*, *what*, and *how*. . . . The issues that must be faced before firm use is gained are:

Does the word 'knowledge' indicate something the organism possesses or produces? Or does it indicate something the organism confronts or with which it comes into contact? Can either of the viewpoints be coherently maintained? If not, what change in preliminary description must be sought?"

In view of what has been said above, readers presumably will not be surprised by the assertion that the significant scientific breakthrough of the present century is man's discovery of a satisfactory and therefore useful answer to the question, What is 'knowledge'? Instead of using this form of the question, including that unsatisfactory word 'knowledge,' however, we can pose the question as follows: How can we be sufficiently confident that an assertion is warranted to justify using such a warranted assertion in solving the problems of men. And the answer to this question may be summarized: Such confidence is justified when the allegedly warranted assertion is the outcome of applying certain well tested methods or procedures in conducting inquiry.

Col. Harwood's conclusion to his article:

The door has been opened to a revolutionary advance in inquiries into the behavioral sciences. Through that door man may advance in finding solutions to the problems of men in society. Given time, a few decades at least but perhaps a few centuries, there may be sufficient progress to insure the survival of the best that western civilization has developed through its long and troubled past. We and our immediate followers now are in a far better position to learn how we got where we are, how it happens that civilization has flowered as it has here in the United States, how the new nation that was to be the hope of the world, that inspired and still is inspiring the struggles of men to break out of the bonds enslaving them, how that nation has succeeded to the extent that it has, and perchance how all men may move forward to a better world. From improved understanding of the behaviors of men in society we may reasonably hope for what men have sought since time began, not an Utopia of plenty and slothful ease but a civilization that will foster in every possible way the development of individual men to their maximum capacities and the firm establishment of a good society.

CHAPTER FOUR
THE 1960S:
A DECADE OF TURBULENCE; THE COLONEL VS. UNCLE SAM

The turbulent 1960s were the decade of civil-rights protests and changing social mores; of a generation gap dividing the popular culture of young and old in music, dress and attitude; of ethnic pride movements, and anti-war protests; of a continued Cold War ranging from a growing bloody conflict in Indochina to a race to be the first to land a man on the moon. It was the age of Martin Luther King and Malcolm X; of the Beatles and Flower Power; of Neil Armstrong

A shirtless drummer and a floral dress-wearing flutist jam during the Woodstock music festival, in upstate New York, 1969.

An astronaut plants the U.S. flag on the moon.

in his spacesuit declaring, "That's one small step for a man; one giant leap for mankind." It was a decade of general economic prosperity, but social divisions that tore at the fabric of American society.

The decade began with a swelling of the middle class and economic growth marked by a rising gross domestic product. John F. Kennedy, sworn in as president in 1961, signed the biggest tax cut in U.S. history after taking office. About $200 billion in war bonds matured, and the ongoing G.I. Bill helped create an educated workforce. A gradual shift toward globalization could begin to be felt, as Europe and Japan were

U.S. choppers supporting ground troups during the Vietnam conflict.

Civil rights leader Dr. Martin Luther King. Jr. (left), meets activist Malcolm X in the halls of the U.S. Capitol, in 1964.

well in recovery after the ravages of World War II, and the United States developed a trade deficit. American banks began lending dollars to foreign governments and businesses.

As U.S. military involvement in Southeast Asia developed into a full-scale war, federal government spending fed the military-industrial complex. Meanwhile, the legacy of President Franklin D. Roosevelt's New Deal manifested itself as the government funneled huge funds into social programs that were part of President Lyndon B. Johnson's "Great Society" programs to eliminate poverty (hovering at about 19 percent of U.S. households) and racial injustice by addressing urban problems, improving transportation, and increasing government funding of education and social welfare programs, including Medicare and Medicaid.

By the end of the decade, the growing toll of American military involvement in Vietnam, and government spending on social programs, was draining government coffers and dividing society. And the steamroller of economic growth was slowing.

AIER GROWS AT HOME — BUT LOOKS TO EUROPE FOR FUTURE

FOR AIER, BIG CHANGES were in store — on and off campus — during the volatile decade. In 1962, the Institute opened its 10,000-square-foot research library (formally dedicated in 1975 as the E.C. Harwood Library). In 1968, three additional staff houses were built east of the library. The Institute also weathered one very serious storm. A group of AIER faculty members had organized an investment advisory division at the Institute, which was giving financial advice and earning income. That prompted the Internal Revenue Service, in 1964, to revoke AIER's tax-exemption status. It was a critical blow. The Institute had mailed its circulars, newsletters and books at the lower nonprofit U.S. postal rates. AIER also had operated pooled income funds. Factions developed among the faculty over whether to change AIER's mission. But loyal followers of the original mission — including voting member Roy Anderson Foulke,

Sr., a vice president at Dun and Bradstreet and a personal friend of Col. Harwood, prevailed. The necessary articles of amendment to AIER's corporate declaration were signed in February 1965 — creating a separate for-profit investment-advisory service (American Institute Counselors) and bringing the Institute in line with the Internal Revenue Code's Section 501(c)3 for charitable nonprofit organizations. AIER also created a board of trustees. The disgruntled faculty members left the Institute.

In this decade, great developments would also take place abroad for the Institute, as Col. Harwood pondered whether his native country had turned too far away from its original ideals — and the very freedom it had so long promised and nurtured were in peril of disappearing forever. In 1968, AIER's stalwart founder retired as AIER director (although remaining as treasurer) and moved to Lugano, Switzerland, where he intended to found several investment corporations meant to allow loyal clients of AIER's subsidiary, American Institute Counselors, to invest in

gold and protect their assets. In Switzerland, in 1972, he would, indeed, set up the Progress Foundation, to investigate the influences that cause progress or regress in civilization. Col. Harwood also made plans to move permanently to Switzerland should his position in America become politically untenable due to his constant assailing of federal monetary policy.

He and some colleagues also formed the Behavioral Research Council for Scientific Inquiry into the Problems of Humans in Society. The organization became known by the acronym BRC, and two books it published — *A Current Appraisal of the Behavioral Sciences*, and *Useful Procedures of Inquiry* — enjoyed successful sales. (AIER absorbed the BRC in 1984.)

While anti-government radicals during the turbulent 1960s drew close scrutiny from the federal government, Col. E.C. Harwood — a true patriot who had served his nation in two wars — felt worried about governmental interference with his efforts to educate the public about fiscal soundness. When he founded the Progress Foundation in Switzerland, he stated two

CHAPTER 4

> " The actual order of successful inquiry seems to be: awareness, observation, partial description, conjectures leading to further observation, etc., until an adequate description has been formulated. Descriptions of a small part of the full sequence may be mistaken as the key to the whole process; e.g., when inquiry is understood as beginning with a 'well-formulated' hypothesis and then searching for evidence, or when mathematical transformations are assumed to be the essence of scientific inquiry, or when logical deductions are emphasized. "
>
> — *From* Useful Procedures of Inquiry, *by E.C. Harwood and Rollo Handy, 1973.*

reasons for organizing it:

1) Future possible interference with freedom of inquiry in the United States was foreseen.

2) The new and distinctively American line of advance by Charles Peirce and William James, John Dewey and Arthur Bentley might thus be taken to Europe, from which most developments in philosophy had come to the United States. There was at least a possibility that later in the United States the return wave of a newly developing epistemology might become more widely applied if supported by importations from the traditional sources of philosophy in the Western World.

In the years ahead, the Progress Foundation would come to own Mondial Commercial Ltd., a Liechtenstein corporation with offices in Lugano, Switzerland, that would allow American investors to put savings into gold by a complex set of transactions. The *Wall Street Journal* and *Fortune Magazine* reported on this investment setup in the early 1970s. It would not be long afterward that agents of the U.S. Securities and Exchange Commission were committing a great deal of time and energy in scrutinizing what Col. Harwood was up to. ❖

HOW INQUIRY PROCEEDS

The "transactional approach" pioneered by American philosophers John Dewey and Arthur F. Bentley, and spelled out in their 1949 book, *Knowing and the Known*, profoundly influenced the research and analysis methodology of the American Institute of Economic Research.

In 1973, the AIER's subsidiary, the Behavioral Research Council, published *Useful Procedures of Inquiry*, co-authored by E.C. Harwood and Rollo Handy. The book included the text of *Knowing and the Known*. Harwood's and Handy's book included an orientation section for the reader that summarized some of the major, but tentative, conclusions the authors reached about inquiry into inquiry:

How Inquiry Proceeds

1: The inquirer becomes aware of a problem situation.

2: He observes some facts that appear to be pertinent. Various aspects and phases of the situation are differentiated, some changes among them are measured, and a tentative partial description of what is happening is begun.

3: In noting connections among some of the things observed and measured, other connections may be imagined. The inquirer focuses on what seem to be the pertinent aspects and phases of the situation, and develops a conjecture as to what may happen under specified circumstances.

4: That conjecture may involve other facts to be observed, perhaps including some facts originally not believed to be pertinent. As the inquirer proceeds, he may find that the original problem situation is quite different than it first had seemed.

5: The tentative description of what happens is supplemented and perhaps revised. Transformations via verbal or mathematical logic may be used. What were earlier taken as facts may be revised or rejected.

6: Perhaps another conjecture occurs to the inquirer about possible connections among the facts, including measured changes.

7: Investigation of the new conjecture requires further observation and perhaps results in the development of a more adequate description. These procedures of observation, reconsideration, renewed observation; i.e., the interweaving or reciprocal stimulation of what are sometimes called empirical observations and the formulation of hypotheses, may be repeated many times in succession.

8: Finally, if the inquirer is successful, a description adequate for resolving the immediate problem situation is developed.

9: Future inquirers may further supplement the description of what happens; in some instances new inquiries may reveal aspects or phases that force drastic amendment of the best earlier description.

10: Inquiry has no necessary end. A *complete* description of even a simple problem situation apparently never has been achieved and may never be, but an adequately useful description is the goal of modern scientific inquiry.

The actual order of successful inquiry seems to be: awareness, observation, partial description, conjectures leading to further observation, etc., until an adequate description has been formulated. Descriptions of a small part of the full sequence may be mistaken as the key to the whole process; e.g., when inquiry is understood as beginning with a "well-formulated" hypothesis and then searching for evidence, or when mathematical transformations are assumed to be the essence of scientific inquiry, or when logical deductions are emphasized.

If the interweaving of observation and tentative descriptions that has been so productive in past inquiries is departed from, the verbal and mathematical transformations used by the inquirer may not be applicable to the data involved. Many inquirers have endeavored to achieve useful descriptions by means of extended verbal logic, or by mathematical transformations not closely connected with observable data, or by the computer models that have become popular (by means of which so-called "theoretical construction" and the mathematical transformations have been mechanized or automated). Some of the displays of technical proficiency may be

CHAPTER 4

impressive, especially to those less skilled in mathematics, but there is little evidence that useful scientific inquiry has been advanced thereby, and there is much evidence that such elaborate theorizing lends a false appearance of authenticity to assertions that by no means are scientifically warranted.

FRED HARWOOD:
FOUNDER'S SON HAS DEVOTED HIS LIFE TO THE INSTITUTE

Trustee and former secretary Fred Harwood grew up at the Institute, and after military service forged a career at AIER.

Fred Harwood remembers an idiosyncratic habit of the man whom he has idolized his entire life: "Dad always carried a gold coin in his pocket. If he ever showed insecurity to me, it was having that little resource right where he needed it, all the time."

Fred's father, Col. E.C. Harwood, was Fred's early mentor in the ways of the world, his counselor as Fred matured, his role model for idealism, integrity and courage, and later his object of undivided loyalty as the elder Harwood fought a harrowing U.S. government campaign to dismantle the American Institute for Economic Research, and to put Col. Harwood behind bars.

The gold coin, though, revealed a vulnerable side to the man whose public persona conveyed utter self-assurance, austerity and ramrod uprightness. The coin may have served as a token of sorts, symbolizing gold's enduring value as the U.S. dollar suffered, decade after decade, from government-instituted inflation. Perhaps the coin was an object of protest against the federal prohibition of U.S. citizens owning gold. But the deepest reason Col. Harwood carried the gold piece may have been more prosaic: He never wanted to be caught flat broke. An impoverished childhood had scarred him.

In his youth, Edward Crosby Harwood had slaved away in odd jobs, such as carting coal cinders out of steep cellars, to earn money for college — only to see his own mother confiscate his savings. He'd grown up with the gold standard, and often had been paid in small gold coins.

"As long as I knew him, he always carried something of true value with him," Fred said.

THE INSTITUTE INADVERTENTLY BECOMES A LIFELONG CAREER

THE VALUE OF GOLD, and its indispensable worth as U.S. currency chronically deflated, would be just one of the lessons Col. Harwood instilled in his children. But earlier than that came a lesson on working for wages.

Fred, his older brother, William, older sister, Eve, and younger sister, Katherine, grew up in the Castle on AIER's estate, which the Institute had purchased and begun renovating in 1945. When Col. Harwood and wife, Helen, moved their family from the Institute's previous home, a renovated fraternity house near Harvard's main campus gate in Cambridge, AIER's resident staff moved right along with them like an extended family.

"I grew up with 20 aunts and uncles," Fred recalled with a laugh. "The ground floor was nothing but businesses and the kitchen and dining room. The mailing room, the faculty office, dad's office, the accounting office were all on the ground floor. Our family had a suite of four rooms on the second floor."

Outside lay piles of rocks, boards and masonry left from construction of the great stone house that had only been 90 percent completed. Col. Harwood had a bulldozer brought in and he cleared much of the debris by pushing it down over a hill (where the rubble remains to this day). But an immense amount of work lay ahead to put the house and immediate grounds in livable order. The staff and family members all pitched in. Pebbles packed the soil, preventing grass from growing. "As soon as I was old enough, I'd take my little red wagon and start putting rocks from the front lawn into it and carrying them down around the corner, at a dime a load," Fred said.

His jobs at the Institute continued for the rest of his growing-up years — emptying wastebaskets, installing plumbing, digging ditches. "I learned the application of scientific method by passing tools to dad and others as they maintained and improved the facilities," Fred said. "I began studying AIER's *Research Reports* as after school I tended the printing press in the basement. When I was 14, dad gave me my own underlined copy of John Dewey's *Human Nature and Conduct*, a gift I actually read as I puzzled over dad's singular generosity."

By the time Fred was in high school, he'd decided to pursue a career in the construction industry. After graduation in 1962, he enlisted in the Army and was assigned to heavy-equipment school. His training surpassed that. Stationed in Germany, he earned certificates in heavy-equipment instruction and repair. He also served as the nuclear, biological and chemical warfare officer for his platoon. And, beating out candidates who were master sergeants, Fred was awarded a position as technical inspector determining eligibility for repair or replacement of multimillion-dollar engineering equipment that supported U.S. missiles on the border of West and East Germany. The tremendous responsibility the Army placed on his shoulders rapidly matured him, and as his three-year commitment was six months from conclusion, Fred contemplated forging a career in the Army.

Ironically, his father — a retired Army officer who'd served in both world wars and had volunteered, unsuccessfully, for the Korean conflict — persuaded Fred to leave the service. Gen. Lyman Lemnitzer, Supreme Allied Commander for NATO, was an old West Point classmate of Col. Harwood. Col. Harwood had been making personal visits to Europe, scouting for a site to build a second institution modeled on AIER. On one of these trips he met with Lemnitzer. Neither patriot was pleased with the growing U.S. military involvement in Southeast Asia. "They were of the old school — if you went to war, you didn't put men, material and money in harm's way without committing everything to winning that war," Fred said. "And Lem told dad that there would be no honor in Vietnam. He said that in 1964."

Fred returned to Great Barrington with his wife, Michelle, and a son, Kirk, born in Germany. The family moved for the time being into one of AIER's upper-story apartments in the Castle, while Fred made plans to start a heavy-equipment company. But an emergency led him to put his idea on a backburner.

"One of the letter shop people at AIER walked off the job," Fred recalled. He himself had plenty of experience in that end of the Institute's operations, since he'd run the press from age 14 on through his high school years, after school. "I got that temporary job," Fred said. In time, a succession of other jobs at the Institute sidetracked his goal of founding a construction company. Every time he was ready to move ahead with his business idea, something else came up at the Institute. He ended up serving in posts such as production manager, and administrative director.

In the end, Fred never started his company. "Looking back at it, different things happened at different times," Fred said with a chuckle. "I stayed at the Institute 41 years."

SON PROVES TO BE A KEY ALLY TO THE COLONEL

COL. HARWOOD CERTAINLY BENEFITED from having his youngest son apply his talents to the Institute's work. As the 1960s unfolded, AIER's founder grew increasingly anxious about the dollar's devaluation and the federal government's guns-and-butter spending. The

Marshall Plan to reconstruct postwar Western Europe had left vast quantities of greenbacks in Europe. Domestic social programs promulgated by the Democratic Party threatened to further deflate the dollar's value, as did the steadily ratcheting up of the U.S. military presence in South Vietnam. On top of those worries, Col. Harwood — a longtime critic of federal monetary policies — sensed that he, and the institute he'd founded, could end up in the crosshairs of a governmental vendetta.

He began searching for a place outside the United States in which to base a new institute, to carry on AIER's cause and guard against the day that AIER's position in America became untenable. He traveled several times to Europe to locate a likely site. Fred was on military leave, in France, with his father on the November day in 1964 when presidential election returns from the United States showed that Lyndon B. Johnson had beaten Republican nominee Barry Goldwater. "That was the first time I ever saw my father cry," Fred said. Col. Harwood knew LBJ's programs — which fell under the umbrella that came to be known as "The Great Society" — would create an even larger economic problem for America.

In the late 1950s, Col. Harwood had taken his family on vacation to Switzerland. He remembered the beautiful lake and mountain area around the financial center of Lugano in the far south. Indeed, it filled the bill. The Swiss constitution was based on the U.S. Constitution. The plaza in downtown Lugano had a statue of George Washington. Another attractive attribute: The Swiss banking system protected the secrecy of its depositors.

In addition to seeing how overprinting was debasing the dollar, Col. Harwood noticed that the price of gold was beginning to rise, a nickel or a dime at a time. AIER's affiliate, American Institute Counselors, provided investment counseling and brokering. While it was illegal for U.S. citizens to own gold, Col.

E.C. Harwood with 11 grandchildren, 1967.

Harwood formulated a plan that could facilitate American investors buying gold, or gold stocks, and then protect their assets in Swiss banks. And so, in Switzerland, he incorporated Progress Foundation and a subsidiary named Mondial.

A great many AIER supporters in the United States were as worried as Colonel Harwood about losing their assets to runaway inflation. They became subscribers to the investment entities Harwood set up. After the U.S. Congress legalized the right for U.S. citizens to own old British sovereigns, Col. Harwood availed investors in Mondial the opportunity to buy these gold coins on the foreign markets and have them kept in mass-deposit storage in the Swiss Credit Bank. The bank's vaults filled up with an avalanche of sovereigns. Then Mondial started selling metric accounting units — each unit equal to 1 gram of gold. U.S. investors would send Mondial money; whatever the gold price was in London's market at the end of the day when money was sent, the investor owned that amount in gold bars, which was stored in the Swiss Credit Bank. The investor received a paper receipt.

E.C. and Helen Harwood at AIER, 1965.

Then Col. Harwood lined up a third investment avenue: buying Swiss real estate. He contemplated a community of terraced apartments on a mountainside outside Lugano, and named it Monte Sole. Swiss lawmakers, alarmed at increasing foreign ownership of their land, changed laws so that non-Swiss could only have extended leases. Col. Harwood then built another community, of condominiums, called Falçieu. Tenancy soared.

Mainstream American media began writing of Harwood's success in leading investors to gold. In the early 1970s, he enjoyed a measure of celebrity in financial circles, was dubbed, "the grandfather of gold," and was pursued to do radio interviews from wherever he happened to be on the planet.

And about that time, the U.S. Securities and Exchange Commission developed a powerful interest in the Colonel.

SEC agents decided that Mondial's metric accounting unit certificate, showing an investor's ownership of grams of gold in Zurich, Switzerland, qualified as a security — and an unregistered security, at that. SEC agents built a case against AIER and AIC, and sued both, alleging violations of securities law.

In November 1975, SEC investigators showed up at AIER's headquarters in Great Barrington and began going through files, copying materials. Col. Harwood was in Switzerland. He stayed put. If he returned to the United States, he'd be arrested on charges of selling unregistered securities.

For the next several years, Col Harwood and wife, Helen, lived abroad. Their main connection to goings-on back home was Fred Harwood. He became his father's confidant. He also published a newsletter, *The Phoenix*, in Montreal, Canada, to keep investors informed.

"I was willing to execute anything he needed done," Fred said.

AFTER THE SEC STORM, PLENTY OF WORK REMAINED

THE SEC DEPOSED BOTH Fred and his brother, Bill, who was then AIER's treasurer. They were grilled in the Federal Building in Springfield, Massachusetts, over the course of several days about AIER's activities, and those of Mondial.

The SEC sought to dismantle Mondial and return its assets to U.S. investors. The Swiss told them no dice. So the SEC seized the Swiss Credit Bank branch in New York. The Swiss folded, agreeing to certain demands, including liquidation of Mondial and return of money to American investors, who won the choice of repatriating their funds, or not.

Col. Harwood's legal fees ran into the millions of dollars. His lawyers were able to separate AIER, and its reserved life income funds that supported it, from the investigation. And so, in the end, AIER survived. AIC's board chose to settle with the SEC — and AIC separated permanently from AIER. In failing health, and seeing no end in sight to the legal struggle, Col. Harwood finally agreed to a settlement, in 1976, that dissolved the investment entities in Switzerland. The investors in Mondial had seen their assets grow. Not all were pleased to see the opportunity taken from them.

Col. Harwood returned to Great Barrington, to find a board depleted by resignations of trustees

The AIER staff, 1962. E.C. and Helen Harwood are in the second row, center.

cowed by the federal case. But the faithful had remained. AIER's mission would continue.

And Fred, by now his father's righthand man, became his personal editor as Col. Harwood continued penning articles. Fred's wife, Michelle — who had handled a number of tasks at the Institute, including managing the library — became her father-in-law's private secretary.

They knew the Institute's work would carry on, even after Col. Harwood passed on in December 1980.

Fred served as secretary of AIER corporation from 1996. After retiring in 2006, he joined the board as a trustee and was named chairman of the audit committee. He and Michelle live about 10 miles from the Institute to which they made career-long contributions. Neither of their two children worked at AIER — but have carried on family traditions. Kirk, a third-generation Harwood to serve in the military, was an Air Force captain and is now employed as a flight test engineer for the Department of Defense at Edward Air Force Base, California. Kim, inheriting her grandfather's proficiency with numbers, is a CPA and partner in an accounting firm in Great Barrington.

Times change. As AIER reached its 75th anniversary, the federal government no longer seemed concerned by the Institute's views. "Economics is no longer Keynesian, outright, although there are still an awful lot of socialists in academia, but it kind of is restricted to there," Fred said. "We're back to more of a market-oriented economy. We still have a small degree of inflation. The government is less interested in AIER than it probably ever was."

His father's dream for the Institute remains very much alive — offering financial education to benefit the taxpaying citizen. Or, in Fred's words, "A plethora of information that is just so self-evident that people could pick it up and go" — finger snap — "'Of course.'"

The man who habitually carried a gold coin in his pocket "was aiming at public education more than being a policy wonk or having the Institute outright trying to change governmental policy," Fred said. "He said, 'You can do the political things, try to influence policy. But that makes you one of them. The safer thing to do is to not bypass the citizen. Try to give the citizen as much information as possible to be a proper citizen, and let him sort it out.'

"He really did believe in the American experiment. You need to make sure the taxpayer, the person who is really in charge of the future of the country, sets policy, not rich, overpowering bureaucracies."

How effective has AIER been, after 75 years?

"We've certainly done an awful lot," Fred said. "We've certainly not completed our task. Dad and I and others have always said that we don't think that AIER will accomplish its goals at any time in the near future. There's going to be plenty of work as far as we could see."

CHAPTER FIVE
THE 1970S:
STAGFLATION AND INFLATION; AIER OUTLASTS THE SEC

A strange funk permeated much of American society and the economy in the 1970s — a transitional era that saw the U.S. currency move from specie-backed to fiat, and a phenomenon known as "stagflation" emerge. Indelible images from the decade include lines of automobiles snaking around gasoline stations, after oil-producing Arab nations imposed an oil embargo on the United States and other Western powers after the 1973 Arab-Israeli war; Richard Nixon becoming the first president to resign from office, making a tear-filled speech broadcast on live television amid the Watergate scandal; U.S. Army helicopters airlifting American military and civilian personnel and South Vietnamese civilians off the roof of the U.S. embassy as North Vietnamese troops were taking Saigon, ending the Vietnam War; and U.S. embassy employees in Tehran, blindfolded, paraded in front of TV cameras by Iranian students holding them hostage.

The portmanteau "stagflation" entered economists' common vocabulary as inflation persisted alongside stagnant economic growth in the United States and other industrialized and developing countries. This macroeconomic problem belied the prevailing Keynesian school's view that held it unlikely that inflation and stagnation would occur simultaneously. The reality of stagflation meant government leaders could effectively employ neither traditional response to the respective problems — expanding the monetary supply or fiscal policies to battle slow economic growth; or contracting the monetary supply or tightening credit and governmental spending to reduce inflation.

Cars lined up for fuel at a gas station during the oil crisis of 1973.

In 1971, President Nixon sought to increase demand for U.S. goods abroad and devalued the dollar — pulling the United States out of the Bretton Woods system, ending the dollar's historic convertibility to gold, and letting the currency float on world markets. Yet the supply shocks of oil-production cuts from foreign suppliers resulted in large part in chronic stagflation throughout the decade.

If the idealistic 1960s was the age of the "We Generation," the 1970s was that of the "Me Generation." The book, Looking Out for Number One, *topped best-seller charts in 1977. Nihilistic disco music and punk rock ruled the pop-radio airwaves. Cynicism seemed to replace the characteristic American trait of optimism — a point President Jimmy Carter emphasized in July 1979 during his heartfelt address, after the Organization of Petroleum Exporting Countries had boosted oil prices yet again, sending the cost of gas at the pumps skyrocketing and leading to major shortages and the boiling over of Americans' frustration over a seemingly interminable economic decline. Carter's approval rating in polls stood at 25 percent — lower than Nixon's during the Watergate scandal. "In a nation that was proud of hard work, strong families, close-knit communities and our faith in God, too many of us now tend to worship self-indulgence and consumption," Carter said. "Human identity is no longer defined by what one*

Night clubs in the late 1970s attracted party animals known for a fondness for disco music, gold chains and cocaine.

does but by what one owns."

He continued: "For the first time in the history of our country a majority of our people believe that the next five years will be worse than the past five years," Carter said. "Two-thirds of our people do not even vote. The productivity of American workers is actually dropping, and the willingness of Americans to save for the future has fallen below that of all other people in the Western world." He continued, "We remember when the phrase 'sound as a dollar' was an expression of absolute dependability, until 10 years of inflation began to shrink our dollar and our savings. We believed that our nation's resources were limitless until 1973, when we had to face a growing dependence on

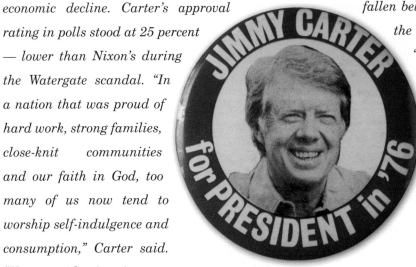

1976: Campaign button for Democrat presidential candidate Jimmy Carter.

foreign oil. These wounds are still very deep. They have never been healed."

Carter intended his words to be a pep talk to reverse citizens' crisis of confidence in government and society; but the address became popularly known as "The Malaise Speech." The next year, Republican presidential nominee Ronald Reagan defeated Carter's reelection bid in a landslide.

A BATTLE AGAINST THE 'SUCKERS' ENTRAPMENT COMMISSION'

AIER SURVIVED ITS MOST perilous decade ever. Much of the danger came from a lawsuit filed in 1975 by the U.S. Securities and Exchange Commission against AIER and its then affiliated investment-counseling service, American Institute Counselors, Inc. The legal battle over alleged violations of securities laws — and related to corporations Col. Harwood set up on behalf of investors wishing to invest in gold-related contracts in Switzerland, and even to have Swiss bank accounts and apartments — was resolved in 1976. AIC's board chose to settle with the SEC — leading to AIER separating

> **"They're a lousy bunch of buttinskies."**
> — *Investor Millicent Hull, referring to SEC investigators, in an interview with the* Wall Street Journal.

permanently from AIC.

Col. Harwood maintained that his Swiss-based Progress Foundation and its affiliates were outside the SEC's jurisdiction because the assets were in Switzerland. Harwood himself waged a valiant fight against the agency he dubbed, a "Suckers' Entrapment Commission." He even petitioned the U.S. Congress to take action against the SEC for what Harwood alleged were the agency's numerous violations of law, including ignoring limits of statutory authority, abuse of subpoena power and even a cover-up. Finally, he agreed to a settlement that returned investors' overseas funds to them, dissolved the foreign entities, and had him refrain from acting as an investment adviser or engage in investment-company activities. In a moral victory, investors won the right — over the

> **"You can get Equity Funding's and Penn Central's glossy reports, all audited by CPAs. But the world has changed; now you have to find honest men. If people aren't satisfied with the integrity of the trustees of the Progress Foundation, we ask them not to bother us, please. We're just not interested in dealing with people who can be so silly as to think an auditor's report will protect them."**
> — *Col. E.C. Harwood, in an interview with* Fortune Magazine, *1974.*

> **❝**We will meet the Commission in any forum, on any ground, because we are convinced that an unbiased, knowledgeable and thorough examination will convince any intelligent observer that not only are we NOT a group of 'tough, often seemingly depraved malefactors,' to quote Chairman Sommers, but that, on the contrary, the advice and analysis of AIC has provided perhaps the only way that one can hope to preserve the fruits of his labor.**❞**
>
> — *Col. E.C. Harwood, in a 1976 statement to the U.S. Securities and Exchange Commission, on behalf of AIER, AIC, and the investment entities he'd set up in Switzerland.*

SEC's objection — to swap their gold-mining stocks to a U.S.-registered mutual fund whose portfolio included gold-mining securities or to have the stocks transferred to their private accounts in Switzerland.

At AIER, an air of uncertainty hung over the staff, unsure whether federal agents could show up and padlock the doors at any time. The pressure from the SEC's witch hunt separated the faithful from the fair-weather. The board of trustees divided into two factions, with one remaining loyal to Col. Harwood in absentia, and the other blaming him for placing the Institute at peril. A law firm hired to represent AIER in the ongoing SEC investigation insisted the board give it a mortgage on Cotswold — the house and the 100-plus acres — in order to guarantee his fee. Some trustees wanted to go along with that, but the opposing faction shot down that proposition. A number of trustees, ultimately fearful of federal reprisals against them, resigned from the board. The remaining members, casting their lots with Col. Harwood, never lost their faith in him or the Institute's mission, and formed a strong core that, as time went on, guaranteed the Institute's survival.

'LEAN YEARS' LED TO A STRONGER INSTITUTE

FRED HARWOOD TERMED THIS period "the lean years" in a speech he wrote in March 1986 to deliver to the voting members of the corporation. An excerpt:

"When in 1968 Col. Harwood retired to worldwide business, he left the Institute (AIER and its subsidiary, American Institute Counselors) in the capable hands of its [officers] C. Russell Doane and James T. Gibbs. For about six years, the Institute celebrated increased earnings and status among readers, the media, and employees. From about 1974, however, when the Securities Exchange Commission began to question the legality and propriety of Institute operations and its ties to Col. Harwood's overseas operations, results have been mixed.

"Aside from the SEC's punitive actions, probably the most influential event was Russ's heart attack and subsequent death. Left without a tough, seasoned leader while Col. Harwood was relatively isolated in Switzerland fighting unprecedented violation of Swiss banking secrecy, the Institute became prey for diverse interests ranging from those of the SEC to those of a clinical maniac. To make matters worse, others cultivated a growing schism among employees, officers, and trustees.

"Before Col. Harwood's death in December 1980, at tremendous cost to the Institute and its supporters, the SEC gave up its witch hunt with a reprimand and the promise from everyone never again to sin. In the meantime, AIER had selected its third leader, created a presidency, evicted AIC, and installed a successor advisory, American Investment Services.

"All of the above events recreated an Institute unlike its predecessor. On the one hand, its voting membership and board of trustees contained many new persons. Both boards had grown accustomed to intervening in Institute daily affairs. Clients and other interested parties had formed protective committees who were relatively close to operations here. Many employees had made personal sacrifices on behalf of Col. Harwood, the Institute, and others.

"On the other hand, the 1970s had seen the fruition of decades of Institute cautions. As economic events proved the value of Institute research and recommendations, it gathered many late 'fairweather friends' as new clients and subscribers. And the rapid turn of events had repopulated Institute employee ranks. Management policy and technique both fragmented and changed due in part to internal frictions and in part to inadequate structural control over the successor advisory." ❖

CHAPTER 5

No predictions of market movements ever are offered. On the contrary, the impossibility of successfully forecasting market trends, even as long as ordinary business cycles, is stressed frequently. One result is that its subscribers do not include a large percentage of brokers' offices needing to generate commissions. A second result is that AIS publications do not appeal to the millions of investors who are addicted to chasing stock-market fluctuations.

— Col. E.C. Harwood, on the mission of the newly formed American Investment Services, 1978.

A FEDERAL WITCH HUNT ENDS IN A PYRRHIC VICTORY

In November 1975, one day before Thanksgiving, the U.S. Securities and Exchange Commission sought an injunction against Col. E.C. Harwood, five associates and the various investment and educational entities he'd founded in Switzerland and Lichtenstein. These entities were set up to allow U.S. clients to invest in gold and otherwise protect their assets from a perilous domestic environment that threatened their wealth through inflation, taxation and dismal opportunities in the stock market.

SEC lawyers went so far as to seek out a federal judge at his home on Thanksgiving Day and persuade him to sign the court order barring any transactions of the holdings. In the midst of an 18-month investigation, the agents claimed they were seeking to prevent losses in some $150 million in gold, gold-mining stocks and other gold-related assets held in Swiss bank vaults by some 3,500 U.S. investors. The 72-page complaint alleged that Col. Harwood, American Investment Counselors, the foreign entities he'd founded and the Swiss bank that stored investors' assets had operated "in near total disregard for and in violation of virtually the entire panoply of federal securities law."

As *Barron's* reported, "The phrase referred chiefly to the activities of Colonel Edward Crosby Harwood, alumnus of West Point, economic theorist, civil engineer, perennial partisan of gold and sworn enemy of the SEC. Even before the Colonel had taken to damning the agency by name, he was attacking the ideas by which it lived. For 40 years, against all odds, he argued the case for economic liberty and the international gold standard, opposing government meddling, Lord Keynes, paper currencies and, on most investment matters, nearly all the sages of Wall Street."

THE COLONEL VOWS A FIGHT TO THE FINISH

IN RESPONSE TO THE SEC's investigation, Col. Harwood promised a fight to the death and released a statement on behalf of AIER, AIC, himself, and the entities he'd set up in Switzerland. The prologue attacked each main issue the federal agency had raised:

"We challenge the SEC staff to find one single instance in which any trustee, officer, or employee of any of the organizations which are the objects of this investigation, has in any way directly or indirectly diverted funds to his own use or benefit.

"We challenge the SEC staff to find one single instance in which any funds invested as a result of the recommendations of AIC have been used in the way which Commissioner Sommers (quite properly) finds offensive.

"We welcome the SEC investigation, we do not fear it. We will place the record of AIC, in terms of the success of its recommendation, beside that of any investment advisor.

"We welcome any intelligent comparison to our record, and we are convinced that a fair and responsible investigation into our activities will only demonstrate that those following our advice have indeed been able, to a great degree, to preserve the economic fruits of their labors, even in the face of inflation and depreciation of the currency.

"We will meet the Commission in any forum, on any ground, because we are convinced that an unbiased, knowledgeable and thorough examination will convince any intelligent observer that not only are we NOT a group of 'tough, often seemingly depraved malefactors,' to quote Chairman Sommers, but that, on the contrary, the advice and analysis of AIC has provided perhaps the only way that one can hope to preserve the fruits of his labor.

"We have opened every file belonging to AIC and AIER to the Commission staff. There is nothing to hide and we welcome a public investigation.

"We are unique among organizations in that all of our efforts are devoted ultimately to serving as scientific advisors and researchers in the field of economics. Because we believe we are unique, we are skeptical that the investigation conducted by SEC staff to date has resulted, or given its nature, could result, in an overall understanding of our goals, aims or activities. We believe that only in direct face-to-face discussions with the Commission itself can this understanding be obtained. Obviously, such a confrontation is not within the framework of a usual SEC enforcement investigation. We invite the Commission, and its Commissioners, to meet with us, to break out of its accustomed mold and to recognize that unusual situations require unusual procedures."

Intense SEC pressure followed against the defendants, including Swiss Credit Bank, and the Swiss government. The AIC trustees eventually caved in, its board choosing to settle with the SEC. Col. Harwood fought on, retaining nine lawyers in five cities and shelling out about $25,000 every month in legal fees. In December 1975, the Swiss government blocked his personal safe-deposit box and his wife's family's trust account, which were in Switzerland, where the Colonel and wife, Helen, resided. For seven long months, until the Swiss restored access to the accounts, the Harwoods survived on Social Security, Harwood's Army pension and contributions from supporters.

ATTACKED ON TWO FRONTS, THE COLONEL ACCEPTS A GRUDGING TRUCE

AFTER THE SWISS BANKING Commission determined that funds held in Swiss accounts for the entities Harwood created "do not meet Swiss requirements," Col. Harwood reconsidered his vow to battle the SEC to the end. "There is no possibility of getting a determination on the merits of the case now that the Swiss government has capitulated," he told the press. "The basic issues will never be tried," he said. "I thought I was fighting with a wall at my back. But then there were two fronts with corresponding legal costs." He noted, too, that he was 76, with a record of heart trouble, and the odds were not favorable for a man in his condition to withstand a possible three-year process of trial and appeal.

At the beginning of August 1976, Col. Harwood became the final defendant in the case to settle with the SEC. As *Barron's* reported: "He promised to refrain for life from selling securities, engaging in business as a broker-dealer and dispensing investment advice. He pledged, moreover, not to tell a lie or withhold information if he should chance to offer, purchase or sell any security. He promised to cooperate with the court, and swore that he had entered into the agreement voluntarily, without promise, threat or duress. He neither admitted nor denied the charges against him and vowed not to attempt to influence or control events in Switzerland as they relate to the case."

The SEC put aside its complaint with prejudice. Col. Harwood issued a press release saying, "The SEC has not established any aspects of the 72-page complaining against Harwood. Implications in SEC publicity releases last November that records might have been destroyed and that funds might have been misappropriated or be inadequate to cover obligations have proven to be without justification."

Assets from the foreign accounts were distributed to their U.S. investors. The SEC sought to have investors' South African gold-mining stocks transferred to U.S. Treasury notes, but investors instead won the right to exchange them for shares in a U.S.–registered mutual fund that included gold-mining securities, or deposited in their own private Swiss accounts.

While the SEC considered its work a victory for investors, the *Wall Street Journal*, in an article of May 16, 1978, reported a different angle. The article was headlined, "Some Investors Say SEC Did Them Dirty By Suing Gold Enthusiast in Their Behalf." An excerpt:

"And did these well-meant efforts win the undying gratitude of the gold investors? Far from it. Instead, the SEC seems to have earned their undying rancor; many of them in their 70s and 80s blame its intervention for robbing them of needed income.

"'They're a lousy bunch of buttinskies,'" says Millicent Hull, 79, of Ringoes, N.J. Mrs. Hull, a retired real-estate agent, says she invested her entire savings, $10,000, in an annuity plan called the Metric Accounting Unit Storage Agreement, one of 10 complex investment devices attacked by the SEC complaint. Rightly or wrongly, she blames the commission's intervention for a sharp drop in her annuity payments. She says she has had to abandon a dream trip to the Pacific Northwest in her mini-motor home.

"We have become the real injured parties in this action," adds Edward Ahrens of Princeton,

N.J., a retiree who used to own a physicians' billing service. "It seems to me that all of the injuries that the SEC accused the defendants of causing us were done to us legally by the officials acting in this case."

'MR. DOOM & GLOOM: HOW A PESSIMIST MAKES HIS CLIENTS RICH IN GOLD BY PREDICTING DISASTER'

The *Wall Street Journal* dispatched a staff reporter to Great Barrington in 1973 to report on Col. E.C. Harwood's unorthodox investment guidance. Here are excerpts from the article, published in May of that year:

Operating out of a stone mansion that he purchased in 1946 and a low-slung annex built subsequently, Mr. Harwood — "Ed" to old friends and "Colonel" to others — and a staff of 10 investment advisers manage portfolios of about 600 clients. The assets of individual clients range from under $50,000 to over $6 million. Altogether, the portfolios are valued at over $250 million, the Colonel estimates.

Since the start of 1972, during a period when many U.S. investors have seen their assets shrink drastically, the value of portfolios managed by American Institute Counselors has about doubled.

How does the Colonel do it? What is his secret? What hot stocks does he know about? The answers to the three questions are: 1. pessimism. 2. gold. 3. none.

Americans and Gold

It's illegal, of course, for Americans to buy gold bars. But coin ownership is allowed. Until very recently, the Institute recommended such purchases . . . But it now is felt that most coin prices have reached levels that make them much less attractive than, say, in 1970 when a British sovereign sold at $9.90, or less than a third of the current level. . .

Mr. Harwood has recently set up an arrangement by which clients can purchase so-called metric accounting units rather than still more gold coins. What a client may do is buy a contract with dollars or other currency that may later be cashed in, again, for dollars or other currency, but is measured, both at the outset and termination, in terms of grams of gold. Thus, for example, if the dollar price of gold goes up in coming months, a contract buyer would be able to cash in his contract for more dollars than he paid for it. The contracts, though recommended by American Institute Counselors, are actually offered by Mondial Commercial Ltd., which as a Swiss company isn't prohibited from owning gold. Mondial charges a small fee for the service. These contracts haven't been challenged by U.S. authorities, but some people think the contracts are tantamount to owning gold bars and thus eventually will be challenged by the U.S. government.

PRESERVING THE AMERICAN EXPERIMENT — IN SWITZERLAND

When *Fortune Magazine* published an article, "Gold Bugs Are on the March," in its June 1974 issue, one of the proponents of investing in the yellow metal whom *Fortune's* reporter interviewed was Col. E.C. Harwood. The magazine article noted that Harwood was the guiding force behind American Institute Counselors, an offshoot of the American Institute for Economic Research. The magazine reported that AIC now had some 650 "'continuous supervisory clients' who paid up to three-tenths of 1 percent of their assets annually to have the Colonel, or one of 12 account supervisors on staff, watch over their investments."

Fortune Magazine printed this photo of Col. Harwood in its June 1974 article, "Gold Bugs Are on the March."

The article noted that the number of AIC clients had jumped more than 50 percent since 1971, and continued, "The reason for the boom is clear. For the past two years AIC has been steadily recommending that clients put all their assets into gold-related investments, reserving a small portion for silver coins, 'savings deposits for emergencies,' and, for the elderly, annuities denominated in Swiss francs."

The reporter interviewed a satisfied AIC client who enthusiastically said his portfolio had quadrupled in two years. The article reported: "One of his investments has been a remarkable instrument recommended by AIC and known as a 'metric accounting unit.' Apparently designed to get around the prohibition against Americans' owning gold 'directly or indirectly,' the unit seems to operate like a mutual fund in precious metals and mining-company stocks. The minimum investment is $10,000. An investor sends the money to Swiss Credit Bank in Zurich, but simultaneously enters into an agreement with another organization, Mondial Commercial Ltd., a Liechtenstein corporation with offices in Lugano.

"The wording of this agreement is not without ambiguities, but clients interpret it to mean that their return on this investment will vary with the price of gold. It is also their understanding that, upon demand, they can receive the present gold value of their original $10,000 in any currency of the world; e.g., if the price of gold were to double, after the original investment was made, the investor could receive $20,000 (less fees)."

AN OPPORTUNITY TO OWN GOLD, CLOAKED IN SECRECY

MONDIAL COMMERCIAL LTD. WAS just one entity that Col. Harwood put together in Switzerland in an overall strategy of providing safe havens for clients' investment dollars. In his mind, the stock-market was toxic, the U.S. government and the banking system continued to allow inflation to rob individuals of their wealth, land was too risky an investment because taxes could be raised at any time, and gold — the historic commodity of commerce — was logically the best investment. But the U.S. government prohibited its citizens from owning the yellow metal other than in coins. Thus, Mondial — whose system of allowing U.S. citizens to invest in gold was cloaked in secrecy. The *Fortune Magazine* article reported:

"One confusing aspect of this arrangement has to do with Mondial's technique for satisfying these potential claims. Mondial says that it is not buying gold with U.S. investors' funds — if it were, U.S. citizens could not legally invest in the m.a.u.'s. It seems likely that the organization is buying other precious metals, whose price might be expected to move with that of gold.

"Since AIC does not provide any financial information about Mondial, an investment in metric accounting units requires a lot of faith. Mondial is entirely owned by something called Progress Foundation, which was founded last year in Switzerland, with Harwood's encouragement. The purpose of the foundation is to conduct research "on the advance and retardation or decline of civilizations." A majority of the foundation's 13-man board of trustees are Swiss citizens, but four, including Harwood, are with the Great Barrington group.

"That representation, says Harwood, is all the protection anyone should want. He recoils from the notion that investors would feel more secure if they could at least see Mondial's financial statement. 'Listen, you can get Equity Funding's and

Col. Harwood in front of San Salvatore Mountain in Switzerland. The photo was taken from the fifth floor of the first building for Mondial investors, above Lugano.

Falçieu, where AIC clients could maintain long-term residence, was set in a majestic Swiss alpine setting.

Penn Central's glossy reports, all audited by CPAs," he says calmly. "But the world has changed; now you have to find honest men. If people aren't satisfied with the integrity of the trustees of the Progress Foundation, we ask them not to bother us, please. We're just not interested in dealing with people who can be so silly as to think an auditor's report will protect them."

AN ARRAY OF ENTITIES SET UP TO PROTECT CLIENTS

IN ADDITION TO MONDIAL (which, in fact, maintained British sovereign and Australian gold coin sub-accounts at Swiss Credit Bank, one of that nation's three largest banks) and the Progress Foundation (set up as a Swiss charitable, educational foundation, and which served as an umbrella organization controlling the other entities), the protections that Col. Harwood arranged for his loyal clients included:

- World Economic Research Trust Registered: a Liechtenstein charitable organization that purchased, on behalf of clients, annuities payable in Swiss francs from the Swiss Life Insurance and Pension Company. WERTREG earned a 3 percent commission from Swiss Life, but returned that earning to the client save for one-tenth of the commission (0.3 percent of the purchase price), which was paid to American Institute Counselors as its standard advisory fee.

- Friends of American Institute for Economic Research Fellowship Fund Trust: A trust fund that received loans on demand notes from AIER in the Institute's role as trustee of pooled-income Reserved Life Income gifts. The Friends Fund, as it was known, purchased gold stocks.

- Monte Sole: A planned small town near the major banking center of Lugano in the scenic south of Switzerland, near the Italian border, characterized by lakes and mountains. Here, Progress Foundation was to be centered, and clients could acquire long-term leases on homes in Monte Sole. But environmental issues prevented building permits from being obtained, and subsequent changes in Swiss law regarding foreigners owning Swiss real estate kept Monte Sole from being developed. Monte Sole took the funds that had come from prepaid leases and purchased gold stocks on behalf of its clients.

- Falçieu: A concept similar to Monte Sole, its apartment residences were completed and most of them were occupied by 1975.

In the denouement of the Securities and Exchange Commission's investigation, the aggregation of entities was dissolved and assets transferred out of Mondial's funds to other funds for the investors.

CHAPTER 5

'WHY AIER?'

The September 1976 *Economic Education Bulletin* included an article that contrasted AIER's research methods with those of other economic schools. Ernest P. Welker, the Institute's acting director, penned the piece in advance of delivering the words the following month to AIER's board of trustees and corporate members.

Excerpts from the article:

Scientific Procedures of Inquiry

To state glibly that the scientific method of inquiry is at the foundation of our work has the virtue of being concise, but it has the weakness of being relatively uninformative. Therefore, I shall expand on what we mean by these procedures of inquiry and how we apply them. . . .

First, we are not engaged in the quest for "certainty," or the pursuit of TRUTH. If either of these have meaning (we do not deny the possibility), at this stage of development we are not aware of what the meanings are, and we have concluded that we would be wasting our time in searching for them. Therefore, we do not seek, and do not think we have ever found, absolute, perfect, or final solutions to economic problems. We must always hold open the possibility — no, probability — that our descriptions of economic relationships and our assertions about their implications might be inaccurate, either in detail or even fundamentally. For this reason, our publications contain many qualifying words, such as "seems to," "probably," "apparently," "presumably," and so forth. Such words might seem to be equivocations to some readers. Or, readers might feel uncomfortable with them, because such words might suggest that we do not know what we are talking about. (I think persons most dislike uncertainty. Many evidently can accept quite easily bad news, but they find uncertainty highly frustrating and frightening.) The state of economics as a science at this time is such that *there are severe* limitations to the understanding of relationships and, therefore, to the accuracy of predictions. In fact, there is little, relatively speaking, that we (and we think others) can assert with substantial confidence.

Let me return to the matter of TRUTH. If we have abandoned TRUTH, or absolute certainty, as the goal of inquiry, how is the accuracy of assertions and descriptions to be assessed? Does every assertion have the same validity, or warrant, as every other assertion? We think not.

Our substitute for the goal of certainty (our "yardstick" for judging the validity of assertions) is that of useful descriptions of *what has happened and probably will happen under specified circumstances*.

How does this goal enable one to assess the validity or accuracy of assertions? Or, what does the adjective "useful" designate? It designates:

Descriptions that can be tested by replicating the work as much as practicable to see if the evidence confirms or refutes the description.

Descriptions that enable one to predict what will happen and that allow one to assess how closely the predicted events conform to what actually occurs.

Predictions that facilitate adjusting behavior so as to accomplish some objective.

Our procedure presents some severe difficulties in not taking *perfection* as the goal or in not asserting that one has reached it. For example, we must admit that an alternative description might have been *more useful*. Humility is a necessary characteristic of a scientist. He must be willing to have his assertions challenged; indeed, he must be ready to help test their accuracy or even refute them; thus, we have the "humble" goal (the scientist's goal) of trying to report (without distortion or ulterior motive) what has happened and probably will happen under specified (limited) circumstances.

The few relationships that we have been able to identify as providing a basis for adequate prediction are quite limited, particularly with respect to timing. For example, our study of the statistical indicators of business-cycle changes enables us to forecast the direction, but not the magnitude, of the trend of general business activity for about six months ahead. The usefulness of this information probably varies considerably among our readers. Stock-market traders will find it very little help at all, since changes in trends of common stock prices lead changes in the business cycle; therefore, they presumably "discount" a recession or expansion in advance. However, businessmen might find our forecasts useful to the extent that their business activities are cyclical.

Sticking with the Evidence

The quest for "certainty" is a widespread aspect of human nature. Much inquiry has been directed toward that end. Einstein, for example, accomplished his highly important and useful work prior to about 1920 and spent most of the rest of his life, I believe, looking for something called the Unified Field Theory that he thought would reconcile apparent inconsistencies among various useful descriptions in physics. Einstein never found the "truth" he was looking for. He was a scientist and observed the facts. That he could not describe the facts fully and in ways that satisfied him presumably was a great disappointment to him, but he "stuck" with the facts just the same.

The objective of attempting to avoid distortion or bias is an integral part of applying scientific procedures. Since our objective is to try to understand how economic developments are connected in order to ascertain what adjustment behavior might lessen or solve the problem, IT IS NO HELP TO ATTEMPT TO MAKE "FACTS" FIT ONE'S CONCLUSIONS. Just as underlying supply and demand conditions eventually overwhelm attempts to "rig" markets, so do events eventually reveal the error of inadequate descriptions, no matter how vigorously those descriptions are asserted.

An alternative procedure to altering one's assertions to conform to the evidence is to "reinterpret" the assertions of a "great man." This often has been done when facts did not appear to conform to the predictions made in *Das Kapital*, *The General Theory*, or even the *Wealth of Nations*. This practice apparently is based on the assumption that some persons are blessed with special insight; therefore, discrepancies between "theory" and facts must result from erroneous interpretation of the great man's theory. Persons using this procedure evidently believe that if assertions are repeated often enough, the nonconforming evidence eventually will disappear.

For example, Keynesian theory, which has been adopted by a great many economists, is one type of insistence of accuracy through repeated assertion. Such repeated assertions, however, do not help to correct the errors involved by one iota. Oppositely, that these repeated assertions have been harmful is quite evident today.

Another type of intentionally distorting reports is revealed by recent attempts at a UNESCO-sponsored conference of Latin American nations to establish a governmental agency to control the dissemination of news, and thus to allow only "good news" — as viewed by these governments — to be published. The notorious rewriting of history in some Communist nations, in which former "heroes" have been demoted, sometimes into nonexistence, is another example. Economists on occasion also have attempted to rewrite history, sometimes somewhat "successfully." Again, consider how Keynesian theory ostensibly was supported by the "facts."

Some who disagree with AIER findings may view our work as also biased, but we try very hard to eliminate bias and to make ongoing improvements in our instruments of research. For example, we have not regularly printed results of our work on the Harwood Index of Inflating for some time, because we have had doubts about the warrant of some techniques used in compiling data for that index. Recent monetary developments (such as the introduction of NOW accounts, better techniques of managing cash, and the large amount of fiat dollars now used outside the U.S.) are some reasons for this doubt. If we were concerned primarily about our "image," we would not have suspended publication of this index. We would have continued as before, but who would have benefited from that?

In terms of making a major contribution to further generations, simply putting into print and thus disseminating reports of historical data with a focus not found elsewhere could be the "key" that later might "unlock" alternatives to the then-dominant theory of how events were connected. Such work might lead to correction of totally controlled views about economic relationships that had been supported only by carefully "selected" but inadequate data.

AN IMAGE AS GOOD AS GOLD

The front of the Harwood Gold Piece, issued by Gold Standard Corp. to commemorate E.C. Harwood's campaign for the right of U.S. citizens to own gold.

The year before Col. E.C. Harwood's death in 1980 at the age of 80, his lifelong career on behalf of sound money, sound economics, and sound scientific procedures was recognized by an oversubscribed minting of the Harwood Gold Piece: a 1-ounce standard gold coin bearing his likeness. It was a fitting honor for the man who had campaigned long and hard for the right of U.S. citizens to own gold — taken away in 1933, and restored by Congress only 41 years later (after the breakdown of the Bretton Woods Agreement). In fact, Col. Harwood was hailed as the "George Washington of the modern sound-money movement" by the Gold Standard Corp. of Kansas City, which issued the coin.

The back of the Harwood Gold Piece.

In its first year of minting, the Harwood Gold Piece sold 5,094 coins. Col. Harwood had allowed the minting only after his supporters agreed to insert the words, "American Institute for Economic Research" on one side, and, "For integrity there is no substitute" on the other. The coin was the first commemorative gold coin issued in a series by the Gold Standard Corp. and a Rhode Island mint honoring classical economists such as Adam Smith and Friedrich Hayek.

Many more bullion-grade Harwood coins were struck over several years and mostly subscribed to by AIER's many long-term friends and supporters. At the time of minting, Col. Harwood and Queen Elizabeth of Britain were the only living persons whose likenesses were on gold coins. The mint-proof coin was double-struck for a mirror finish and frosted likeness. All coins were minted from standard gold coin alloy of 95 percent fine gold (1 ounce), plus 3 percent copper, and 2 percent silver.

A LETTER TO PRESIDENT FORD

THE AMERICAN INSTITUTE COUNSELORS, Inc., ran a full-page advertisement in the Sunday *New York Times* of Nov. 17, 1974. Under a title, "Restoring Economic Order," the ad began, "That the United States and most other leading industrial nations are confronted with serious economic disorder is clearly apparent. Perhaps the most alarming symptom is the increasingly rapid decline in the buying power of currencies, that is the accelerating upward trend of most prices."

The article argued for returning the U.S. dollar to the gold standard, among other drastic corrections to the economy. Accompanying the ad was an open letter from E.C. Harwood to President Gerald R. Ford. The letter:

The President
The White House
Washington, D.C. 20500

Dear Mr. President:

Most economists are in one of four major groups. For the last three decades, Keynesian economists have dominated the field and have been the principal advisers to governments and central banks. They have relied on what may be called secular revelation and related older procedures as their methods of inquiry. Based on their theories they have urged perpetual inflating to perpetuate prosperity.

Some economists are "monetarists" or "Friedmanites." They also advocate continual expansion of the domestic money supply at some definite rate without limit or restriction by international money-credit developments.

A third group are the classical economists who rely on procedures of inquiry developed about 2,000 years ago but now largely superseded.

A fourth group rely on modern scientific procedures of inquiry developed during the present century. Much of the work of the National Bureau of Economic Research that was done under the guidance of Dr. Wesley C. Mitchell until his death (but not more recently) reflected application of these procedures of inquiry. The work of American Institute for Economic Research during the past 40 years also reflects application of these procedures.

The group of 21 economists selected for your "Summit" conference includes 12 Keynesian economists (most of them educated at or connected with Harvard). Of the 21, nearly all of them have had advisory or administrative experiences in the Government where they have been, in varying degrees, the architects of the economic disaster now confronting Western civilization. These include some "Friedmanites."

Dr. Greenspan, of your Council of Economic Advisers, is perhaps the only classical economist you will be consulting.

Of the modern economic scientists developed at the National Bureau and at American Institute for Economic Research the list of 21 includes none. The latter in particular for the past 40 years has been publishing Research Reports in which economic developments have been analyzed and the present economic turmoil has been predicted.

Would it not be wise to consult some of the modern economic scientists in the field of economics?

Sincerely,

E.C. Harwood

E.C. Harwood
Director Emeritus

DR. ROBERT C. WEEMS:
A STEADFAST SUPPORTER FOR SIX DECADES

Dr. Robert Cicero Weems, Jr., began reading publications from the American Institute for Economic Research while serving, in 1939, as the nation's youngest business-school dean (at age 29) at Mississippi State College in Starkville. Weems, the son of a bank president, had been investing in the stock market since age 15, and continued even during the Great Depression while earning his bachelor's degree in business from Mississippi State and a master's in business administration from Northwestern University. He developed expertise in stocks, bonds and investment trusts, and at one point sold some securities at a loss to pay for graduate school at Columbia University, where he earned his doctorate in economics.

Dr. Robert C. Weems has been a longtime member of AIER, and remained as a trustee during the Institute's dark days of the 1970s.

Weems took an immediate liking to AIER's belief in a small federal government, a balanced budget and a sound monetary policy opposing inflation. That placed him at odds with fellow college faculty — who regarded AIER as an oddity, a fringe organization — but his support of the Institute and admiration for its founder and chairman, E.C. Harwood, never wavered. As Weems, who turned 98 in July 2008, recalled, "The Institute's literature that came across my desk seemed very interesting to me, and I developed a strong interest in the organization. I agreed with its critiques of federal monetary policy, and also valued the Institute's recommendations on individual investments, which were extremely conservative."

Weems subscribed to AIER's *Research Reports* and *Investment Bulletin* offering investment advice and remained on the mailing list after leaving Mississippi for the University of Nevada, in Reno, where he was founding dean of the College of Business Administration. He regularly bought the Institute's publications. In the early 1960s, the Internal Revenue Service questioned whether AIER merited nonprofit status and was entitled to tax exemptions. Col.

Harwood called on his friends to help his cause. Weems, as a longtime newsletter subscriber, was invited to join AIER's corporation.

In 1963, Weems became an AIER voting member and began attending the annual corporate meetings. Within a year, he had accepted Col. Harwood's invitation to join the board as a trustee. To this day, Weems harbors great respect and affection for the late Harwood, whom Weems refers to as "the Colonel." After serving a couple decades as an AIER corporate trustee, Weems stepped down from the board but continued on the Institute's investment committee, setting policy for the endowment that eventually surpassed $100 million. Into his 90s, Weems traveled once a year across country from his home in Reno to Great Barrington for the annual members meeting.

The following interview took place in summer 2007:

How did you first become aware of AIER?

I was teaching money and banking. And anyone who teaches those subjects comes almost immediately to the subject of inflation, which is when the government lets too much money get into circulation, and there's more money than goods, and so prices begin to go up. Since I was teaching students to be aware of inflation and trying to get them to understand what was causing it, that's when I ran into Col. Harwood's publications, which came as circulars through the mail to the college of business. I'd used them in my classes. My students mostly liked them. The faculty didn't.

How common a term was "inflation" in 1939?

Most people were not really aware what was happening to them. Not even all the academics were familiar with it. The new Keynesian economics had come along about that time, and its principal motive was that inflation was not all that important, because it said inflation contributed to the flow of goods even though prices would rise. So most people were not particularly worried about inflation, and they welcomed any policy that came along, believing that old-school economics had brought us the Depression.

As you continued receiving AIER publications through the 1940s and 1950s and into the 1960s, what impressed you about the Institute?

The Colonel was an honest individual. Politicians in the government would hail any new economic theories that came along, anything to get votes, and the Colonel was man enough to stand up against the government and say, "Look at all the harm you're doing, printing all that money." And that's when I became attached to the Colonel, because he was independent, a strong individual who could stand up even against the United States government if needed. He saw what was going on was really not best for the country.

What advice did AIER give to the private investor?

This is one of the factors that made the Colonel unique. At the same time he was fighting the U.S. government because the government wouldn't keep itself in a sound economic condition, he was advising his clients how to get rich off the process. He was saying it was a pretty good idea to get your money into gold or silver or copper. It was a good idea to move into common stocks, particularly the very highest grade of blue chips. The main argument was that as the supply of money increases and prices go up, these blue-chip firms' income would go up. The Colonel was more interested in his subscribers preserving their purchasing power than he was in making a hell of a lot of money.

How did you follow his financial advice?

He was recommending gold stocks in South African mines for a long time. He kept constant research on the individual mines. That was his major recommendation, and I followed suit. I made money on it. I also followed his advice on convertible bonds, which have options for exchanging for common stock at a fixed price. I bought these bonds in Pennsylvania Railroad.

How did Col. Harwood, and AIER, survive after the federal government ratcheted up pressure against them?

The Colonel got into trouble with the government, which didn't like the Colonel's criticisms. People in government were sensitive to people who were criticizing what they were doing. The Colonel had an income-tax exemption for the Institute, claiming it was a charitable and educational body primarily. It had seminars for students, it subsidized some scholarships, and it produced circulars and in general was just well known for its stands against the government. The IRS went after the Colonel by denying his tax exemption. Things were getting so hot for the Colonel he was almost being labeled as unpatriotic.

That battle was settled, but the Colonel began looking around for a possible haven if he ever had to move out of the United States. He built a community of apartment houses in Lugano, Switzerland, to rent to his investment clients, and he prepared to set up a new organization like AIER in Europe. The U.S. government didn't like that, and started to claim that the Colonel was advocating the export of capital. But even though he was living abroad during those years, he was determined to retain control of AIER. One of the things he put into the bylaws was a standing committee whose members would be nominated, really, by themselves. The standing committee also was the nominating committee for the board of trustees. So the Colonel, through his ability to control practically everything that was going on through the standing committee, pretty well determined the inflow of talent into the organization. One thing about the Colonel — you better not disagree with him. He always was able to find a manager who understood Harwood and didn't challenge him.

What was your personal impression of Col. Harwood?

He was a very austere individual, just like you'd expect of an engineer who was a colonel and a graduate of West Point. He stood about 6 foot 2, with very straight posture, a little bald, with a low, precise speaking voice. He didn't brag about himself at all. He was just sure of himself. Everybody just had the feeling, when they were around the Colonel, that you were in the presence of someone who was sending messages out to you, just telling you that you're in the presence of a great man. He had tremendous presence.

How proud are you of your membership in AIER?

Extremely so. One reason is its stand for good government and sound money. Another is that I was fortunate to know and work with Col. Harwood over the years. He was really a wonderful guy. Also, I'm proud that my own positions on investing the Institute's endowment led me to be recognized as a sound money man, too.

The Institute has proved itself to be very effective in generating sound research and giving sound investment advice. Quite a few clients, and board members, too, have followed AIER's recommendations. The Institute still is not highly thought of among university economists. They just sort of say, "Oh, it's just one of those appendages you find in any field, kind of a fringe organization." But Col. Harwood's views have stood up well over these 75 years.

AMERICAN INVESTMENT SERVICES: SCRUPULOUSLY OBJECTIVE ADVICE

When AIER founded American Investment Services, Inc., in 1978 — to provide asset-management services to individuals and organizations, and to publish a monthly, eight-page *Investment Guide* newsletter — it gave AIS a similar mission as AIER, which would wholly own the investment service.

Like AIER, AIS would provide information based entirely on objective scientific research on the economy, refusing to sacrifice accuracy simply to find a broader customer market by misleading simplification. A preponderance of investment advisory services and financial newsletter purveyors pitch either over-optimism or impending doom and gloom (or both) to build up clientele, but AIER's research would inform AIS's investment policy, which would be developed and monitored by the Institute's investment committee. AIS would receive no compensation from any third party.

As Col. Harwood wrote after AIS's founding:

"AIER's publications do *not* sacrifice scientific accuracy in the interests of finding a broader market by misleading simplification. AIER does report its findings in plain language without euphemisms intended to avoid antagonizing some readers, but it does not sensationalize or depart from accurate reporting.

"AIS follows AIER's example as is described above and is otherwise different from most investment services:

"No predictions of market movements ever are offered. On the contrary, the impossibility of successfully forecasting market trends, even as long as ordinary business cycles, is stressed frequently. One result is that its subscribers do not include a large percentage of brokers' offices needing to generate commissions.

"A second result is that AIS publications do not appeal to the millions of investors who are addicted to chasing stock-market fluctuations.

"Unlike nearly all newsletters and investment services, neither AIS nor AIER rent or sell their lists of subscribers and former subscribers. For many of the popular investment services, income from name rentals is the principal source of profit."

CHAPTER SIX
THE 1980s:
REAGANOMICS, MARKET CRASH; LIFE WITHOUT THE COLONEL

*C*hunks of reinforced concrete shattered from battering bulldozers and swinging sledgehammers as the Berlin Wall — symbolizing the Iron Curtain, and the Cold War, itself — began inevitable demolition in November 1989, to the jubilation of Germans on both sides of the border. The fall of the wall, an indelible image from the 1980s, presaged reunification of East and West Germany and the tumbling of Communist regimes across Europe, including the disintegration of the Soviet Union in 1991, signifying a Cold War victory by the Free World and capitalism. However, the cost of increased military spending under Ronald Reagan's two terms as U.S. president, coupled with tax cuts in the higher-income brackets, spurred the federal debt to triple in seven years to $2.6 trillion by September 1988, making Reagan the first president in four decades not to reduce debt as a share of gross domestic product.

"Reaganomics" — the popular term for the economic policies promulgated by Reagan and his White House successor, George H.W. Bush — intended to shrink government spending, reduce marginal tax rates, deregulate industry and lower inflation through tighter control of the monetary supply. The U.S. economy, in dire shape as President Jimmy Carter left the White House in January 1981, reeled from a global petroleum shortage and record high prices caused by the disruption of Iranian-produced oil because of that nation's revolution. But from 1981 to '83, a two-year recession and the Federal Reserve's tighter control of the monetary supply and interest rates dropped inflation from 13.5 to 3 percent.

Wall Street was primed for a trading boom — abetted by computer technology. The advent of the personal computer in everyday American life characterized society's quickening pace.

President Ronald Reagan and first lady Nancy had frequent media moments.

IBM launched its first line of PCs, and "Silicon Valley" in northern California emerged as the high-tech hub of the nation, home to leading computer and semiconductor firms and venture capitalists. Stock-market shares began a steady acceleration in prices and trading volume, with computers increasingly carrying out transactions by institutional or large commercial investors and mutual-fund corporations. Programs set computers to automatically buy shares within set parameters; the electronic funds transfer system entered wide usage; arbitrageurs plied their trade with a vengeance.

Three words, "Greed is good," summarized the spirit of market speculation, smugly declared

The New York Stock Exchange hummed with activity during the 1980s market boom.

by actor Michael Douglas in his Oscar-winning role as "Gordon Gekko" in the movie, Wall Street. *Real-life arbitrageur Ivan Boesky partly inspired Gekko's corporate-raider character. Boesky's brazen bets on corporate takeovers earned him a fortune of about $200 million before the U.S. Securities and Exchange Commission took him to task for insider trading. He dutifully cooperated with investigators and informed on several cronies — including Michael Milken, the pioneer and major purveyor of high-yield, non-investment-grade "junk bonds." Each man paid heavy fines and served prison time.*

Investors not privy to privileged information suffered through "Black Monday" — Oct. 19, 1987 — when the Dow Jones Industrial Average plunged 508 points, 22.6 percent, the largest single-day drop in history. Similar declines struck markets around the world. Causes of

Col. Harwood on his 80th birthday, Oct. 28, 1980. He's proudly holding a 1-gram Swiss gold bar — sounder than the currency of his native country.

> **❝**The last night of his life we talked at length: how the SEC had been foiled, how the Institute was beginning the long climb up from the devastation of that horrific battle. Promising younger people were taking over the responsibilities, backed up by you, dear friends, whose loyalty had survived the severest testing. Ed died in the pre-dawn hours of Dec. 16, 1980, at peace, his part done. He knew the rest of you would carry on.**❞**
>
> — *Helen Harwood, in a speech to members of the AIER corporation, Oct. 1, 1983.*

the crash remain mysterious and debatable — perhaps related to share overvaluation, program trading or market psychology — but it would take nearly two years for the Dow to regain its previous closing high.

The nation's savings and loan industry experienced a more spectacular debacle during the 1980s. The S&Ls carried large numbers of low, fixed-rate mortgages issued in the 1950s and '60s. The disparity between the income the S&Ls earned on these mortgages and what the institutions paid in interest on new deposits eroded their capital. In 1982, Congress deregulated the S&Ls, letting them invest in areas outside of residential real estate lending. Many S&Ls speculated on questionable ventures, such as oil patches and property developments,

and after the real estate market weakened and oil prices plummeted, more than 200 S&Ls went broke. The Franklin Roosevelt-era Federal Savings and Loan Insurance Corporation saw its coffers depleted. In 1989, The Financial Institutions Reform, Recovery and Enforcement Act abolished the FSLIC, and authorized taxpayer dollars to bail out the failed S&Ls.

Did Reaganomics work? By the time Reagan left office in January 1989, stagflation had drastically diminished as inflation and unemployment had fallen from the rates when he first was sworn in. Critics claimed that the Federal Reserve Board's monetary control, and lower oil prices free of supply shocks, played a bigger role. Keynesians said government stimulation had kept the economy humming.

> **❝**What is worthwhile in life? I suggest that the answer is found not only in carrying your personal and family responsibilities as you should but also in the realization that in some small degree to the extent of your ability you helped to foster a more just social order for those who will come after you.**❞**
>
> — *Col. E.C. Harwood*

THE COLONEL PASSES ON, BUT HIS LEGACY CARRIES ON

FOR AIER, THE FIRST year of the new decade was marked by the passing of the Institute's founder, Col. E.C. Harwood. To his credit, he had set in place a structure that would carry on without him. Yet the Institute struggled.

Fred Harwood commented to voting members of the corporation in March 1986:

"Following Col. Harwood's death and the subsequent decline in gold and related assets, the Institute entered five lean years of leadership, purpose, and income. In fact, it recently consumed its ready reserves, avoiding a managerial recommendation for a mortgage by the timely death of another RLI donor or final beneficiary.

"Recently AIER restructured its bylaws to give the president acting as shareholder more direct organizational control over the subsidiary advisor. AIER has produced several new booklets that have mitigated the drop in income from falling memberships and subscriptions. AIER and AIS have raised prices and increased mailings. These developments could make 1986 a very good year, perhaps one that will begin restoring operational reserves." ❖

'FROM LITTLE ACORNS'

Helen Harwood delivered the following speech at the annual meeting of the members of the corporation on Oct. 1, 1983, marking AIER's 50th year:

"As we enter this, AIER's 50th year, I find myself thinking back to the early days, like now a time of nationwide depression, a similar time and yet a time with fundamental differences. The costs of rent, office equipment and supplies, of getting out booklets and bulletins, to say nothing of salaries, bear little relation to today's prices. After a lifetime of watching Ed achieve the seemingly impossible, I hesitate to say he couldn't have established AIER under today's conditions. However, they certainly would tax even his powers of innovation.

"In the early 1930s, urged on by Dean Bush of MIT to set up a small research organization to study the economic problems of that depression time, Ed brashly took the $200 that he had been paid for articles published in economic and financial journals, and had a few circulars printed offering for $1 a booklet that he hadn't yet written. His office staff were two: me and Gertrude Bedrick, just out of Simmons College, who was to become a valued AIER employee in the years to come. The two of us typed on envelopes names from a mailing list we acquired — I've forgotten what it was. We folded and inserted the circulars, licked the envelopes and the stamps that went on them, and mailed them off, thinking that would probably be the end of it. But when a reasonable number of dollar bills came back with orders for the booklet, Ed got cracking and wrote it.

"'What Will Devaluation Mean To You?' was one of the first to howl about the dangers of inflation, and it received favorable notice in a monthly bulletin put out by the Book-of-the-Month Club. However, not everybody was favorably impressed. An old beau of mine, who took a dim view of Ed's ideas, asked that, when we sold the movie rights to the book, I use my influence to see that he was engaged to play the part of Devaluation!

"With a little money trickling in, Ed made plans for another publication, 'Life Insurance from the Buyer's Point of View,' and advertised for someone to do the research. He was still in the Army, and, although he claimed and demonstrated that the duties required of an officer in peacetime could be taken care of in half a day, statistical research for the projected insurance book would need more than his spare time. An out-of-work MIT grad with a degree in math answered our ad. His wife was expecting, and even the pittance we could offer looked good. So our second project got off the ground. Again the Book-of-the-Month Club commented favorably; not favorable was the reaction of the insurance companies whose policies had wound up at the bottom of our ratings.

"Many of you here have vivid memories of the early Depression years, how people were eagerly looking for work, almost any kind of work. There was no unemployment insurance as yet; the concept of being "over qualified" for available jobs hadn't come into being. Girls with master's degrees from Radcliffe gladly worked for us for $12 a week, and would pitch in and type envelopes and fold circulars and affix stamps along with Gertrude and me. Those with less education usually started at $10. Later on, we'd have 20 or more girls at a time doing various tasks.

"Predictably, turnover was constant, and Ed soon instituted a system of weekly raises for the efficient that was enthusiastically received although, believe it or not, the raises were seldom more than 25 cents. But that would buy the makings of a substantial breakfast or lunch.

"Three or four more men joined the staff at comparable wages. However, with the men a more professional attitude was adopted. It was assumed that they would still be able to eat if they were occasionally asked not to cash their salary checks for a day or two, until more book orders came in. (For the record, while Ed was still on Uncle Sam's payroll, he took no salary from AIER.)

"At first, we operated as inconspicuously as possible out of Ed's office at MIT, where he was an associate professor of military science and tactics. But after a while their mailing department complained that our mailings were gumming up their facilities, and President Compton, amused rather than angry, told Ed he would have to move his little Institute out of the larger one. So we found a small apartment in Cambridge near Harvard Square. The building was in receivership, and they were delirious with joy to get a tenant that could pay (they hoped) $40 a month rent.

"Of course, we needed furniture for the new quarters. The Harvard Economic Society had gone broke giving lousy advice to clients and was selling office equipment. Desks went for $15, chairs for $5,

Helen and E.C. Harwood with daughter-in-law Michelle, picnicking in a meadow in Switzerland, 1971.

typewriters for $25 or less, depending on condition. It wasn't high-quality stuff by any means, but it sufficed. When typewriters went on the fritz, Ed, an engineer, could give first aid. Just compare this with what it would cost today to set up even a very Spartan office!

"Somewhere along the line Ed decided the time had come to launch an investment advisory service, just a bimonthly trio of bulletins aimed at three levels of investing. You could subscribe to any one for $4 a year, to all three for $10. I was horrified; accepting subscription money would obligate us for a whole year! The project would fail, of course, and AIER, still operating hand-to-mouth, could not possibly be in a position to refund for the unexpired part of the subscriptions. I knew Ed well enough to feel sure he would assume such repayment as a personal obligation; it might take years, but he would dip into his own meager resources to do it. I pleaded with him not to undertake anything so silly. How wrong can you be? Fortunately, he went ahead, as you all know.

"Soon more space became desirable, and Ed dickered with the receiver in bankruptcy for a larger apartment. We had reached the stage where it seemed probable that we could afford $50 a month for rent! Finances were still tight, but Ed had established a minuscule line of credit with the Cambridge Trust Company, certainly more by his power of persuasion than on the basis of our balance sheet. This line of credit was usually a few hundred dollars. It helped that, when Ed discovered in an early bank statement that they had made an error in our favor, he had me call it to the attention of the vice president. Mr. Macomber developed an unbankerly interest in our activities, yet I doubt that he ever really knew how closely we skirted the edge of insolvency. However, he did say to me with a wry smile that AIER's was probably the fastest revolving checking account in Cambridge, if not the U.S.!

"Ed kept an 'A Week at a Glance' calendar propped up on his desk. On the left-hand side of each day's space he would pencil in the return to be expected on that day from mailings already made. On the right-hand side he listed bills that could be paid if the day's mail brought in what we thought it should. There were many days when drastic downward revision had to be made; on the rare occasions when the take exceeded expectation, there was wild rejoicing.

"We early learned that news could adversely affect returns from mailings. One such, the abdication of Edward VIII for 'the woman I love,' nearly swamped us. On the basis of very encouraging returns from test mailings to New Process Company's buyers, we had jumped off the deep end and contracted for their entire list, and the whole darned thing came to the desks of prospective AIER booklet buyers the week the world was holding its breath to learn would-he-or-wouldn't-he. Our circulars went unopened into wastebaskets; the return was a fraction of what we had contracted to pay for using the New Process list. Disaster loomed, but Ed's never-say-die temperament — plus, again, his powers of persuasion — came to the rescue. Laying the cards on the table, he got New Process to agree to let us pay their bill in drips and drabs, as we could. We never skipped a payment. Sometimes it was as little as $2, but *something* always hit the desk at New Process when due.

"In spite of such temporary setbacks we continued to grow, and more space became necessary for the labor-saving machinery we were acquiring piece by piece. The apartment building had a large unused street-level basement at its rear. Ed conned the receivers into putting in

partitions and toilets; we would do minor work like painting. Staff members who cared to do so racked up a little overtime with carpentry chores and such. I've forgotten the rationale for painting the cement floor with aluminum paint, but I well remember the blaze of light that smote the eye when employees arrived for work on Monday.

"By 1937 there was reason to hope that AIER was a going concern, and again quarters had become restrictive. In our after-dinner strolls around Cambridge we discovered a boarded-up, three-story, former fraternity house on Dunster Street, a block-and-a-half from Harvard Square and next to the Harvard gym. Finding a basement door unlocked, we barged in and saw that the place had real possibilities, although much would have to be done to adapt it to our needs. However, when Ed went around to the bank that held the mortgage on the place he got the brush-off; the bank wouldn't consider anything near the price he suggested. It looked hopeless.

"Then on Thanksgiving Day a phenomenal amount of snow fell on Cambridge. We whisked around to Dunster Street and again entered the building. Its lackadaisical caretaker had left a skylight open, and three feet of snow had accumulated under it. Ceilings were falling all over the place; nobody in his right mind would consider having anything to do with it now. However, Ed still saw possibilities if it could be bought cheaply enough. At the bank he told them what we had seen and suggested that, as the building appeared to be a total loss for them, we might be interested in buying the land. They looked, and the next day came a letter saying that if our offer was still open, we could have the property. It must have been one of the deals of the decade — a 30-year mortgage at 3 percent for $30,000, as I remember. Eight years later, when AIER made what will surely be its last move, Harvard University bought 54 Dunster Street on its little plot of land for almost twice the price of this Great Barrington property.

"In the late 1930s jobs were still scarce in the building trades. Ed was able to get two men to come up from Washington for very low wages and undertake rehabilitation of the old Georgian-style brick building. There would be office space on the ground floor and staff apartments on the two upper floors. Its basement provided ample room for storage and even a small apartment for a caretaker.

"Then came the war. Reserve officers on our staff were called up; others went to Washington for better-paying jobs. And, of course, soon Ed was sent to England and later to the Pacific. Disenchantment with Cambridge as a place to live had been growing; no longer basically a college town, Cambridge was now a politically corrupt city. The local public schools were inadequate, and we had already decided that we would have to start Billy, the oldest of our by then three children, in a private school used by area-college faculties to educate their kids.

"As many service couples did, perhaps to bolster hope that there would be a future life together, Ed and I wrote back and forth about another move 'after the war.' We each had copies of *Previews*, a catalogue of large estates for sale, and our letters to each other carried across the Pacific many allusions like "number 369, page 65" that must have puzzled the censors. We finally narrowed the suitable properties down to six, all in the Berkshire area of Massachusetts, to look at when he came back.

"In April of 1945 Ed was invalided home from the Philippines, and in May we set off with some furlough gas to investigate the most promising of the old white elephant estates culled from *Previews*. Again, the times were propitious for our needs. The real estate market was still in wartime doldrums. Supplies for renovating were difficult to get, and the properties were being offered for a fraction of the prices they later sold for.

"The one here on the hill was not our first choice, but became so when we saw the condition of some of the others. Circumstances were good for bargaining. And what a series of long, drawn-out sessions ensued! The owner was a shrewd Italian, his wife was a shrewd Yankee, but in Ed they had found somebody who knew the game. Frequently an impasse would be reached, and the three would sit for a half-hour or so, nobody saying anything, each waiting for the other side to reopen the bargaining with a concession. Finally, a deal was made for the stone mansion and 103 acres of land at a price — $25,000 — that, as I have mentioned, was not much more than half what Harvard paid for the Cambridge property and its small plot of land.

"You know the rest of the story — how at first all operations were carried on in the downstairs rooms of the mansion, the two upper floors used for staff living quarters. How, as we continued to grow, the Annex was built, then the Annex-to-the-Annex, in 1962 this research library, and later the staff houses along the road. Perhaps more is still to come — who can see that far into the future? If the need is there, it will be met, I'm sure, although it is too much to hope that the bargains of the past will ever again be available to us.

"For me, whose life and fortune have been tied to those of AIER for decades, it has been somewhat like riding a roller coaster — exhilarating, scary, often both at the same time. But looking back, so much was just plain *fun*. In spite of the tense times, the narrow squeaks, I wouldn't have missed it for the world. It has been a rare privilege to be part of an undertaking that has fought to gain a hearing for sound ideas in this confused world, a struggle that, I think we can say with confidence, has had beneficial effect.

"AIER has weathered some pretty bad storms. As the SEC tried to destroy the accomplishments of decades, sometimes it seemed that better than 20-20 vision was needed to see the 'light at the end of the tunnel,' to quote from the *Phoenix Bulletin*, in that worrisome time, the only unfettered source of news about what was going on. But even in the darkest days Ed never stopped fighting. I think we will all agree that he was unique, the right man at the right time, and it is my great good fortune to have shared so much of his life. However, it seems probable that, even for a person of Ed's creativity and drive, developing an organization that eventually would grow to the present size and scope of AIER would be difficult, if not impossible, in today's 'depression' times of paradoxical high prices and salaries.

"In 1979 Ed learned that the end of his road was near. His reaction was typical of the way he had lived: putting first things first, and tying up loose ends. We had joined the California retirement community of Casa Dorinda, yet he continued to have new ideas, and much was accomplished in the year-and-a-half of 'borrowed time,' as he called it. The last night of his life we talked at length: how the SEC had been foiled, how the Institute was beginning the long climb up from the devastation of that horrific battle. Promising younger people were taking over the responsibilities, backed up by you dear friends whose loyalty had survived the severest testing.

"Ed died in the pre-dawn hours of Dec. 16, 1980, at peace, his part done. He knew the rest of you would carry on."

OBITUARY FOR COL. E.C. HARWOOD, FROM THE BERKSHIRE EAGLE, DEC. 17, 1980

GREAT BARRINGTON — Col Edward C. Harwood, 80, founder of the American Institute for Economic Research (AIER), died early yesterday morning in his sleep, possibly of a heart attack, at his retirement home at Casa Dorinda, Monticito, California.

The controversial economist founded AIER, a conservative market research organization located off Division Street on property overlooking Long Pond, in 1933. Throughout the years, he was a vociferous critic of a U.S. economic policy that inflated the dollar and removed gold as its standard. Over the years, he recommended gold as a most prudent investment.

In 1934, Col. Harwood wrote a rebuttal to the economic theories of John Maynard Keynes, who advised government spending to promote prosperity. Harwood regarded Franklin D. Roosevelt's adoption of Keynesian policies as America's greatest economic disaster.

Fredric D. Rutberg of Stockbridge, Harwood's attorney, said of him yesterday, "He had one of the brightest, sharpest minds I've ever come in contact with. I'm glad he lived long enough to see his (economic) theories vindicated and himself vindicated."

The latter remark refers to a suit filed in 1975 by the federal Securities and Exchange Commission against AIER and an affiliated educational institution, American Institute Counselors, Inc. The legal battle over alleged violations of securities laws was resolved in 1976.

The colorful colonel, who had many admirers and detractors, had characterized the SEC investigators as "junior G-men" working "Gestapo style" during the course of the suit.

In 1979, Col Harwood was quoted in an Associated Press story as stating that his prophesies of economic doom — of the devaluation of the dollar and the subsequent stampede of investors to gold — had come to pass.

Born in Cliftondale, Massachusetts, Oct. 28, 1900, the son of Edward T. and Mary Howe Pinney Harwood, he was graduated from West Point and later earned master's degrees in civil engineering and business administration from Rensselaer Polytechnic Institute.

He served in the U.S. Army during both world wars and was awarded the Legion of Merit and a Bronze Star.

Col. Harwood's career included stints as an associate professor of military science at the Massachusetts Institute of Technology and as U.S. district engineer in Boston. He was the author of many books and articles on economics. He founded several Swiss investment corporations and served as a consultant to the Progress Foundation, which he set up to research "the influences that retard or advance civilization."

He officially stepped down as director of AIER in 1968 but remained as its treasurer until 1975.

After his retirement, he continued to issue monthly dispatches on the economy from his European headquarters in Switzerland and to promulgate his philosophies through a mailing list that included a million addresses.

Col Harwood left Great Barrington for California on Thanksgiving Day after testifying in a libel suit brought in Berkshire Superior

Court by a former director of AIER, James T. Gibbs, against Harwood, the Institute and its current president. The suit was dismissed Dec. 1. In 1979 he was honored as the "George Washington of the modern sound-money movement" by the Gold Standard Corp. of Kansas City, which minted a 1-ounce gold piece bearing his likeness and the Institute's motto, "For integrity there is no substitute."

Col. Harwood leaves his wife, the former Helen Fowle, whom he married in 1938, their two sons and two daughters, William F. and Frederick C. Harwood of Great Barrington, Miss Eve C. Harwood of Pittsfield and

Miss Katherine S. Harwood of Los Angeles, California; and a daughter and two sons by his first marriage to the former Harriet Haynes of Belmont: Mrs. Marjorie Greer of Concord, Edward L. Harwood of Belmont and Richard F. Harwood of Beverly. He also leaves a sister, Miss Doris M. Harwood of Honolulu, Hawaii; two brothers, William P. Harwood of Northhampton and Harry P. Harwood of Alexandria, Virginia; 13 grandchildren and a great-grandchild.

Col. Harwood's son, William, said the family has no plans for a memorial service, believing that the most fitting memorial is his father's life's work.

'IN HONOR OF E.C. HARWOOD'

(From *Research Reports*, Jan. 19, 1981)

Edward Crosby Harwood, founder of this Institute, was a genius in the sense of one who, beyond the capabilities of most, discerned the important from the unimportant, found solutions to problems impeding advance toward the important objectives, and designed and implemented programs for promoting the solutions.

To Col. Harwood the purpose of life was to serve his fellow humans. "What is worthwhile in life?" he wrote. "I suggest that the answer is found not only in carrying your personal and family responsibilities as you should but also in the realization that in some small degree to the extent of your ability you helped to foster a more just social order for those who will come after you." In E. C. Harwood's own phrasing, the "acid test" of any notion is to see if the ideas lead to the intended objective. Application of this test to E.C. Harwood's life's work leads beyond doubt to the conclusion that he advanced social justice in many ways.

Among those who will read this are thousands of persons who credit E.C. Harwood's financial advice for a substantial proportion of the wealth that they have been able to accumulate or preserve through sound investments. Many thousands of others over the 50 years or so of E.C. Harwood's dedicated efforts to helping others by personal financial advice likewise benefited. All such advice was without charge if given by E.C. Harwood as an individual or with a small charge if extended through Col. Harwood's capacity as an employee of either AIER (when AIER gave investment advice) or AIER's affiliated investment advisory in later years. We find it difficult to imagine more concrete evidence of E. C. Harwood's usefulness to his fellow humans than that he helped many producers of this nation to avoid being victims of the inflating-embezzling process in this country and thereby helped them to retain the fruits of their efforts.

Visitors who came to meet him understandably were impressed with the quality of his conversation

Col. Harwood and son Fred, 1979.

as well as his advice. He would quickly focus on the significant issues, modestly "suggest" what might be a solution to the specific problem, and then politely make plain that he had nothing more to say and had to turn his attention to other things. Charge? No charge, but a contribution to AIER would be appreciated, he would reply. Amount? Whatever the visitor decided.

Col. Harwood's generosity began early in his career and continued to his last days. During recent years he received some recognition for his early advice to make gold-related investments, but not in proportion to the acclaim heaped on less successful Johnny-come-lately gold advisors. E.C. Harwood's successful investment advice long predated his recommendation of gold. In the 1950s, he recommended U.S. common stocks. Before that, beginning in the late 1930s, he recommended defaulted bonds that could be purchased at a fraction of their face value but later paid 100 cents on the dollar. All recommendations were based on his assessment of fundamental economic conditions of the time. Sound procedures, he pointed out, revealed solutions to investment problems as readily as to other problems.

What distinguished E. C. Harwood from most others was the degree of confidence he had in his problem-solving procedures and thus in his conclusions. Temporary adverse market trends, even large ones like the 50 percent drop in the price of gold during 1975-76, did not shake him. "Wait," he would advise, "basic economic conditions have not changed." And those who waited, benefited greatly.

THE 1990S:

BULL MARKET AND HIGH-TECH BUBBLE;

AIER NURTURES SOUND SCHOLARS

A robust U.S. economy through most of the 1990s, including the longest bull market in Wall Street history, led some economists to proclaim that the high-tech revolution had fostered a "new economy," heralding the end of the business cycle. Indeed, the economy featured relative stability in growth, inflation, and unemployment. Inflation averaged about 2.5 percent a year — compared to about 4 percent in the 1980s and 6 percent in the 1970s. Unemployment declined, hitting a 30-year low of 3.9 percent in 2000. Gross domestic product rose by 69 percent.

Ironically, the decade had begun under less than auspicious circumstances. The United States was mired in a recession that had been forestalled in the late 1980s by what some economists considered a miracle: burgeoning consumer confidence and heightened spending,

The city of Los Angeles was engulfed in riots in April 1992 after a jury acquitted police officers of beating motorist Rodney King.

perhaps tied to pre-election presidential activity. But by George H.W. Bush's second year in office, sluggish growth and high unemployment prevailed. He'd famously declared during his 1988 election run, "Read my lips: no new taxes." But in 1990 he compromised with

U.S. forces during a live firing exercise in the desert, while training in Saudi Arabia before the allied invasion of Kuwait in the Gulf War, December 1990.

The personal computer proliferated in U.S. offices and households thoughout the 1980s.

and the rise of the Internet as a popular medium (including email), to cellular phones and handheld personal digital assistants that also accelerated the speed and ease of contacts.

The trading volume in S&P 500 index stocks tripled during the decade; the stock market as a whole yielded more than 25 percent annually in the latter half of the decade. The NASDAQ index, full of high-tech companies, enjoyed a 795 percent cumulative 10-year return by the end of the 1990s. Exemplifying investor headiness was the speculative mania that would become known as the "dot-com bubble." Startup companies that offered sales over the Internet of products or services traditionally supplied by brick-and-mortar businesses launched with characteristically well-publicized initial public offerings. Many of them ignored standard business models in favor of seeking market share at the expense of the bottom line. They sought to expand their customer bases as rapidly as possible with an industry creed of, "Get large or get lost." They spent aggressively, funded as they were by eager venture capitalists, and banked on investors' exuberance with initial public offerings.

congressional Democrats and raised taxes to reduce the budget deficit. He soon contended with a far greater crisis: Iraq's invasion of oil-rich Kuwait, and the potential of Saddam Hussein seizing oilfields throughout the Arabian Peninsula. The U.S.-led United Nations coalition that liberated Kuwait in Operation Desert Storm initially generated high popularity ratings for Bush, but the plunging economy turned voters away from him and put Bill Clinton into office in 1992.

The economy recovered and then boomed. Giddy investors viewed the last decade of the 20th century as the dawning of a new age, one they regarded as marked by increased labor productivity powered by advances in information and communications technology — from the widespread use of desktop and laptop computers

President Bill Clinton announces to the press his intention to ask Congress for supplemental funding for the air war over Yugoslavia, at the White House, April 19, 1999.

An archetypical dot-com, Pets.com, sold pet supplies over the World Wide Web, gaining consumer notice with its sock puppet mascot that made guest appearances on network television talk shows and even appeared on a Macy's Thanksgiving Day Parade balloon. Pets.com went from an IPO on the NASDAQ to liquidation in nine months. Similar spectacular failures included Boo.com, an attempt at creating a global online fashion store, which spent $188 million in just six months; and eToys, whose share price was $80 during its IPO, and less than $1.21 months later, when it declared bankruptcy.

Like all stock-valuation bubbles, the dot.com's was bound to burst. Indeed, beginning in March 2000, the stock market started giving back up to 75 percent of its growth from the previous decade.

INSTITUTE BOOSTS FELLOWSHIPS, BECKONS DISTINGUISHED SPEAKERS

AIER's OPERATIONS CONTINUED TO expand in the 1990s. One area was in its fellowship programs geared to provide direct training and financial support to advanced economics students and established scholars.

The roots of these programs actually date back to 1946, after the Institute moved into its new campus in Great Barrington. AIER determined to help develop economic scientists, and established a competitive two-year graduate fellowship for worthy scholars who would study while in residence at the Institute's headquarters. World War II had interrupted the formal education of millions of students, and many candidates for AIER's graduate fellowship understandably lacked knowledge in subjects crucial to any advanced program of economic study. So the Institute's earliest fellowship programs offered scholars a wide range of tutorials in basic English composition and semantics, logic and economics as prerequisites for advanced study.

Another war — the Korean conflict — erupted several years later, interrupting the formal education of would-be graduate scholars. AIER reorganized its fellowship program in the mid-1950s under the administration of the Interfoundation Committee for Economic Scholarships, which was supported by AIER and four other organizations: The Economic Education Institute, the Economic Education League, the John C. Lincoln Foundation, and the Robert Schalkenbach Foundation. The program accepted some 200 undergraduate scholars per year. But each year this effort failed to produce more than a few highly qualified students to

CHAPTER 7

66There are times I see us in the way the monks of the Middle Ages saw Ireland. The Vandals are tearing up the rest of Europe, but at least in the monasteries of Ireland, we can keep the works of ancient civilization alive. I see our role as similar to that in the economic world.99

— Walker Todd, research fellow and AIER summer program instructor

> ❝The summer fellowship gives me a much more historical perspective of economics. In college, I had one class on the history of economics, but all we did was talk about the people more than their ideas. And the scientific method has influenced me to make sure I take everything into consideration when doing research and analysis. I won't ascribe to one particular point of view, one school of thought, and go by that the rest of my life.❞
>
> — *Christa Jensen, two-time summer fellow at AIER*

enter the graduate fellowship program. The reason? The federal government had vastly expanded its support of academic research programs via research grants and scholarships; at the same time, private endowments such as the Fulbright Scholarship and the National Merit Scholarship program put AIER's program at a severe competitive disadvantage. Top graduate students commonly chose to attend prestigious universities offering the most grant money for research projects.

AIER responded by broadening its summer fellowship program to include graduate students and a small number of distinguished undergraduates. Growth was slow, and into the 1970s, in some years the Institute awarded no fellowships. But by the 1990s, AIER's reputation for research and training, and an expanded effort to attract students, had significantly boosted enrollment. Now the Institute awards more than a dozen summer fellowships each year to college economics students. They come to AIER for an intensive four-week period of study near the beginning of their graduate careers. Those demonstrating exceptional potential during the program earn fellowships in absentia for the succeeding academic year, including full or partial payment of tuition, or a monthly stipend.

Students attend seminars at the Institute, share office space in the E.C. Harwood Library and take meals with the staff and visiting senior fellows — affording invaluable opportunities for interaction with world-renowned experts in a wide variety of fields within economics. The students receive training in several major areas, including the methodology of economists, monetary economics, business-cycle analysis and property rights. Overall, the students are

> ❝What you're hoping to do is gradually improve the quality of public policy in the country as the students whom we have taught rise to higher positions in their own universities teaching others, or they may go into the government or the International Monetary Fund or the World Bank, and try to help reform from within.❞
>
> — *Walker Todd, research fellow and summer program instructor*

exposed to working economists in a practical environment contrasting sharply with the purely academic settings of colleges and universities.

In 1997, AIER began sponsoring a visiting research fellowship program for distinguished, established economic scholars, who are invited to spend part of the summer or even longer at AIER, pursing their chosen course of research. The fellows present their findings to AIER's research staff, other research fellows and student fellows, and also communicate their findings to the Institute's general readership in *Research*

University of the Philippines, the University of Lima, and Fudan University (China).

Luminaries stud the list of guest speakers, which includes author George Gilder; emeritus professor C. Lowell Harriss of Columbia University, a former economic consultant to the U.S. treasurer and to the United Nations; professor Edward Kane of Boston College; Marc Miles of Laffer Associates; U.S. Rep. Ron Paul, a 2008 candidate for the Republican presidential nomination; Richard A. Posner, judge of the U.S. Court of Appeals for the Seventh Court, and a

> **"**One of the most important things that AIER does is try to spread economics knowledge to the general public, which doesn't know much about it. When it comes to voting, it's important to know about tax policy, the costs and benefits of everything so you make the right decisions. It's more important than ever to educate the populace. Not even the people in government know economics. Somehow they pass bills.**"**
>
> — *Christa Jensen, two-time summer fellow at AIER*

CHAPTER 7

Reports or *Economic Education Bulletins*.

The fellowship programs have attracted students, researchers and speakers from the most prestigious universities and colleges in the nation, including Brown, Columbia, Harvard, Johns Hopkins, Massachusetts Institute of Technology, Princeton, Stanford, the University of California, University of Chicago, Vanderbilt and Yale. From abroad, fellows have come from Asia, Europe and Latin America, from institutions as diverse as Cambridge and Oxford, the London School of Economics, Rotterdam University, the University of St. Gall (Switzerland), the University of Milan, the

senior lecturer at the University of Chicago School of Law; and Anna Schwartz, of the National Bureau of Economic Research, who co-authored *A Monetary History of the United States* with Milton Friedman.

AIER's fellowship programs follow the hopes of the Institute's founder, E.C. Harwood, whose uncompromised pursuit of purely objective economic research led him to cast a skeptical eye on research funded by governments, which have their own agendas. Col. Harwood well knew the lessons of history: that scientists should not expect unrestricted freedom of inquiry as servants of a government — or any vested interest. ❖

WALKER F. TODD:
RESEARCH FELLOW AND INSTRUCTOR PROMULGATES
A HISTORICAL PERSPECTIVE OF AIER'S ROLE

Since 1995, Walker F. Todd has been a familiar summertime presence at the American Institute for Economic Research. In addition to serving as a research fellow and a conference organizer, he has been an acting director of the Summer Fellowship Program, an instructor with that program teaching on the history and origins of competing theories of properties rights — and an official curator of night-time screenings of movies of historical value, shown in the Institute's TV Room. These movie nights afford Todd, possessed of a rich, projecting voice, the opportunity to perform in one of his favorite roles: erudite lecturer on esoteric points of history, such as the internecine fighting among leaders of the French Revolution.

Walker Todd speaks on the history of property rights in Western thought during AIER's fall 2004 Property Rights Conference.

A scholar with a wide-ranging and fiercely independent intellect, Todd cherishes AIER in the context of a historical mission. "It's important as a refuge, if nothing else," he said. "There are times I see us in the way the monks of the Middle Ages saw Ireland. The Vandals are tearing up the rest of Europe, but at least in the monasteries of Ireland, we can keep the works of ancient civilization alive. I see our role as similar to that in the economic world.

"We make a point of this in our summer program that we teach classical economics. Nobody else does that as a primary mission. By 'classical' I mean Adam Smith, David Ricardo, Alfred Marshall and others. You go into the average university economics department, and they say, 'Don't bother reading that old stuff. Here's the latest econometric model, you should focus on this instead.' So we see our role as maintaining and promulgating the best of classical economic theory, the idea being that it never goes out of style."

Todd, a resident of Chagrin Falls, Ohio, has unique academic and professional pedigrees. He holds a law degree from Boston University and a doctorate in French from Columbia University. He is an attorney admitted to practice in Ohio and New York, and an economic consultant with two decades' experience at the Federal Reserve Banks of New York and Cleveland. A director and program organizer for the Committee for Monetary Research and Education, he was an adjunct faculty member of the Cleveland-Marshall College of Law for 13 years. His numerous published articles for AIER and other organizations have covered the topics of banking, central banking, monetary and property rights, international debt, the International Monetary Fund, and the regulation of the banking system and financial markets.

OPENING YOUNG ECONOMISTS' EYES TO CLASSICAL TRAINING

TODD IS PLEASED THAT AIER's summer program is increasingly attracting distinguished speakers. "In recent years we've succeeded in upgrading the quality of the outside scholars who visit us as speakers in the summer," he said, "people such as Ed Kane, a prominent economist now teaching at Boston College, and Dominic Salvatore, author of the leading textbook on international economics, and director of the graduate program at Fordham. And there's Anna Schwartz, a frequent visitor, who's still active in her nineties as an economist at the National Bureau of Economic Research, and is well known in monetary economics."

Todd is proud that the summer program is training scholars who can make an impact in economics in the years ahead. "One thing we hope our Summer Fellowship Program accomplishes is opening the eyes of a lot of students to classical economics. If you understand classical economics properly, it gives you a constant frame of reference with which to judge almost any problem you confront in economics and finance. The methodology they get also will open their eyes to being more willing to question the way certain investigations or inquiries are conducted, that more issues need to be fleshed out.

"What you're hoping to do is gradually improve the quality of public policy in the country as the students whom we have taught rise to higher positions in their own universities teaching others, or they may go into the government or the International Monetary Fund or the World Bank, and try to help reform from within. We've had a fair amount of success along those lines, especially the students who are alumni of our programs. They're increasingly getting recognitions at the schools they attend, for being superior products who might have been otherwise overlooked."

The Institute's work, meanwhile, is catching the eyes of high-ranking government

CHAPTER 7

officials and top academic scholars, Todd noted. For example, Larry Sommers, secretary of the treasury in the Clinton administration, read AIER's reports. And the Institute's conferences are attracting top-notch experts. The U.S. executive director with the International Monetary Fund spoke at AIER's conference on the future of the dollar. Kenneth Rogoff, former director of the research department of the International Monetary Fund, and a professor of economics at Harvard, spoke at the conference about reforming the IMF and the World Bank.

"We're gaining," Todd said. "Some trustees feel that unless we're quoted on the front page of the *Wall Street Journal* every day, we're ineffective. We're not. We just watch to see the policy change."

WILLIAM F. FORD:
A RUGGEDLY INDEPENDENT THINKER
ON TIMELY ECONOMIC TOPICS, SUCH AS IMMIGRATION

In summer 2007, Dr. William F. Ford spent two weeks as a visiting scholar at the American Institute for Economic Research. A ruggedly individualistic thinker, Ford was attracted to AIER by the Institute's academic independence from influence by funding sources, and what he calls its "serious economic research on important topics" as well as its "market perspective on economic issues and problems, which is the approach I'm personally most comfortable with."

Ford's academic and professional accomplishments are extensive and impressive. An economics professor at Middle Tennessee State University in Murfreesboro, Ford holds that campus' Weatherford Chair of Finance. In his

Dr. William Ford, a visiting lecturer
in summer 2007

four-decade career as an economist, he's worked in nine of the 13 identified career paths for those with an economics doctorate. These include having served as dean of the business school at the University of Denver; president and chief operating officer of First Nationwide Bank;

director of the U.S. Chamber of Commerce; and CEO of the Federal Reserve Bank of Atlanta.

Ford grew up in the Long Island, New York, town of Huntington, attended the highly competitive Brooklyn Tech public high school, served in the U.S. Navy submarine service, and earned his Ph.D. from the University of Michigan in 1965. As an economist, he's become a prolific writer and speaker, penning more than 100 articles (such as, "Has a Quarter of a Trillion Dollar Settlement Helped the Tobacco Industry?" in the *Journal of Economics and Finance*), delivering talks on a staggering variety of subjects (such as a presentation to the Dietician's Association on "The Wage Penalties of Smoking and Obesity"), and appearing regularly as a guest on *CNBC-TV* and *Bloomberg TV*. One of Ford's specialties: grasping the big-picture issues that popular media and some economists miss, such as the economic impact of the World Trade Center attacks.

"Immigrationomics," one of his talks at AIER in summer 2007, concerned the macroeconomic impacts of legal and illegal immigrants on the performance of the U.S. economy. Ford's iconoclastic views on that subject were featured in an AIER *Economic Education Bulletin* article. His conclusions, supported by research, fit well into the Institute's mission of intellectual objectivity.

NUMBERS POINT TO A SOLUTION: REFORM OUR IMMIGRATION LAWS TO REFLECT REALITY

"My paper says there's too much heat and not enough analysis on the issue of the role of immigrants in our economy," Ford explained. "Very few people — including economists who teach in the field — know, for example, that the immigrants who are now in our labor force are a major source of input through our entire economic process. For example, immigrants make up 46 percent of all the medical scientists in America."

What of illegal immigrants, also called undocumented workers? "If you study media reports about what's happening, you can hear the extreme view, 'Well, there are 12 million criminals here whom we need to round up and kick out.' That's an absolutely irrational approach to resolving the illegal immigration issues," Ford said. "For instance, our entire prison system currently holds just over 2 million Americans, and only 10 percent of them are in our federal prisons, with about 250,000 beds. And overall, our prisons are more than 90 percent full. How are you going to add another 12 million inmates?

"And consider the cost. You've got to find the illegals, arrest them, incarcerate them, and then process them. Only then can you even think about deporting them — *if* you can find a place to send them. If you assumed it would only cost $10,000 per person to do those five things, that's $120 billion. And that wouldn't begin to cover the cost, because it doesn't consider all the new prison cells you'd need to put them in. Even if you said you're going to take five years to do this, and only get rid of 2 to 3 million illegal immigrants per year, you're talking about more than doubling the workload of our prison system and our court system. Also, what about the 3 million U.S. citizens — their children — who are dependents of the illegals? Are you going to force 3 million U.S. citizens to leave the country? If not, who's going to take care of their 3 million children? And are those 3 million citizens, mainly healthy young children, a drain or a benefit to our economy, over their lifetime?

"Overall, U.S. immigrants now comprise about 14 percent of our entire labor force. The illegals alone account for 7 million out of 152 million workers in the United States. That's 4.5 percent of the U.S. labor force. They also account for about 4 percent of our gross domestic product. They represent close to half of all the people who know how to put Sheetrock on the wall of any new residence or business building. They're also a huge fraction of all the people who are able and willing to perform stoop labor in the fields, picking strawberries and other produce.

"I don't know a single economist who believes we could get our unemployment rate below 4 percent. So if you take 4 percent of 152 million workers — that's 6 million people who are going to be unemployed no matter what. Given our unemployment rate, this means only 1 to 2 million unemployed workers will be available to replace 7 million illegal laborers. How are you going to replace 7 million illegal laborers with 1 to 2 million from the ranks of the unemployed? Are you going to get unemployed people living in northern cities to go to Florida or California to work in the farm fields there?

"Deporting illegal aliens would cost us about 4 percent of our $13 trillion in annual GDP — that's about a half-trillion dollars worth of our total output."

Ford's solution is changing our immigration laws to meet the labor needs of the U.S. economy. "The people who employ these 7 million illegals are not doing it because they want to participate in criminal activities," he said. "The reason you have so many U.S. employers hiring 7 million illegals is because they need them to do the work. Why not let in as many people as American employers are willing to sponsor and hire? In other words, let the labor market determine how many workers our economy needs to import from other countries. Let it be a market decision."

CHRISTA JENSEN:
A TWO-TIME FELLOW

Christa Jensen, a student fellow in summer 2007.

Christa Jensen had never heard of the American Institute for Economic Research until she was using the FastWeb Internet search engine for college scholarships. AIER's Summer Fellowship Program came up — the first scholarship program pegged to economics that Jensen had found. The chance to reside for four weeks in a "stone castle" and to visit New England excited her. But Jensen didn't harbor big hopes of winning a slot in the four-week program, which would feature intensive seminars in such topics as methodology of economics, monetary economics, business-cycle analysis and forecasting, and property rights. She expected competition to be fierce for the dozen spaces set aside for students entering a doctoral program in economics or a related field, or who had just begun in a Ph.D. program.

Jensen, 21 then, was attending a small school — Middle Tennessee State University, in Murfreesboro — where she was a senior double majoring in economics and Spanish, and captain of the cheerleading squad. She'd only discovered a penchant for economics in her junior year, when she'd taken an economics course as an elective. But that was enough to convince her to switch majors from biology. She now was intent on earning a doctorate in economics and possibly forging a career as a monetary economist in international development, or perhaps as a think-tank researcher.

To Jensen's surprise, an email from AIER two months after her application for the 2006 Summer Fellowship alerted her to good news: She had made the cut, and would be receiving free room and board, $50 a week to pay for dinner, and $250 a week in scholarship money. Actually, a bit of luck had come into play. "My writing sample just happened to be the only thing I had on economics on my memory stick when I needed to print out and send in my application," Jensen said. "It was a paper I'd written for my history of econ course. It was on Vilfredo Pareto. He was one of the first to introduce a lot of mathematics into economics."

Pareto, a French-Italian economist of the late 19th and early 20th century, helped develop the

CHAPTER 7

field of microeconomics, and had famously observed that in Italy, 20 percent of the population owned 80 percent of the property — spawning the term "The Pareto principle," also called "the 80-20 rule." Jensen later learned that her paper had impressed Walker Todd, acting director of the fellowship program that summer. "Walker said, 'Let's invite this person. She knows Pareto is important.'"

AIER'S CIRCUMSPECT APPROACH WILL LAST HER CAREER

THAT SUMMER, FRESHLY GRADUATED from Middle Tennessee State, Jensen took AIER seminars on money and banking, property rights, and thinking like an economist. She soaked up the approaches to economics that were unlike anything she'd been taught in college, absorbing the principles of AIER's research methodology. "The scientific method taught here teaches to take everything into consideration," Jensen said. "To look at everything from every point of view, and figure it out from there."

She also came to appreciate AIER's value as an educational resource for the nation. "One of the most important things that AIER does is try to spread economics knowledge to the general public, which doesn't know much about it," Jensen said. "It's much better if they do. When it comes to voting, it's important to know, for example, about tax policy, the costs and benefits of everything so you make the right decisions. It's more important than ever to educate the populace. Not even the people in government know economics. Somehow they pass bills."

Jensen performed so well that summer that she earned a share of the Foulke Foundation's annual scholarship, given to AIER student fellows demonstrating the highest potential for development as economic scientists dedicated to finding solutions to human problems. Jensen also marveled at the distinguished economists the Institute brought in as speakers. She chatted with Anna Schwartz, the world-renowned economist who, at 91, was still active with a position at the National Bureau of Economic Research. Jensen asked whether it was normal for a woman to be studying economics back when Schwartz was attending graduate school. Schwartz — who'd earned her master's in economics from Columbia in 1934, at the tender age of 19 — said she had no idea where people got statistics saying women were a rarity in the field back then, but there were plenty of women in her classes.

Jensen herself has found gender parity in the field. The dozen students in her graduate school class at West Virginia University are equally divided by gender. As she pursued her Ph.D. in economics with special interests in urban and regional economics, and in monetary economics, she earned a rare distinction: winning an AIER summer fellowship for a second year: 2007. She was eager for the opportunity to gain yet more knowledge unavailable in academia.

"The fellowship gives me a much more historical perspective of economics," she said. "In college, I had one class on the history of economics, but all we did was talk about the people more than their ideas. They don't offer history of thought classes in graduate school. The summer fellowship gave me a better background. And the scientific method has influenced me to make sure I take everything into consideration when doing research and analysis. I won't ascribe to one particular point of view, one school of thought, and go by that the rest of my life."

AIER's influence on Jensen's critical thinking ability was apparent when she delivered a talk on "industry clusters" at the 2007 summer session. Industry clusters are comprised of firms in the same industry that base their operations in the same geographical location and integrate themselves with local institutions such as banks and colleges. AIER's research approach insists on precise naming of terms.

"Places like Silicon Valley came up on their own, and everyone's trying to emulate something like Silicon Valley in their own city," Jensen said. "I don't think the policies they have now are going to work. My presentation was giving people a background on the field of regional economics and how it's treated industry clusters. The biggest problem with studying an industry cluster is nobody has a good definition of exactly what one is.

"Somebody can say, 'Florida has a tourism cluster.' But that's an entire state, and 'tourism' is so broad. Does it include someone selling T-shirts? Somebody else will say, 'This town has two car factories. We have an automobile industry cluster.' But it's not integrated. It's hard to do anything when you don't have a good definition."

ELAINE TAN:
SAVORING AIER'S INDEPENDENT SPIRIT OF INQUIRY

When Elaine Tan was preparing a paper to deliver to a summer seminar at the American Institute for Economic Research in 2006, a catchy title presented itself. Her topic was whether the truck system, in industrializing Britain, exploited workers by paying them wages in kind, including advances in cash and company-store goods. The issue bore contemporary relevance because the International Labor Organization, a specialized United Nations agency, criticized the paying of wages in kind, citing the historical British example.

In an AIER seminar that summer, lecturer Walker Todd sang a classic country song, *Sixteen Tons*. One of the phrases in the lyrics caught Tan's ear, and it became her presentation's title: "I Owe My Soul to the Company Store." She went on to give her presentation, concluding that the truck system did not lower British wages by as much as was popularly believed, the system's credit to workers at least equaled credit terms elsewhere, the system was mutually beneficial, and evidence doesn't support abolishing similar practices today. The "company store" doesn't necessarily possess employees' souls.

Tan — an economic historian on the faculty at Royal Holloway College, the University of London — enjoyed her research fellowship and returned to AIER again in summer 2007. "I don't like academia that focuses too much on the theoretical and ignores what's really going on in the world,"

Dr. Elaine Tan, a research fellow in summer 2007.

she said. "This is not the case at AIER. There are no boundaries in terms of intellectual issues. You can say what you want and can believe what you want, but you better back it up. You'll get questioned, 'Do you have data to back it up?' 'Are your directive propositions logical?' 'Are they sound?' 'Do they fit into the real world as seen from the past, i.e., historical perspective, or right now?' That's what attracts me."

A native and citizen of Singapore who is a permanent resident of the United Kingdom, Tan earned a doctorate in economics from Cambridge University. After working on the faculties at Oxford University and the University of Michigan, she took a position as an economic historian at Royal Holloway. Technically speaking, Tan was a civil servant in Britain, a servant of the state. "Not very many people would dare to speak up against their employer," she noted.

CHERISHING THE INSTITUTE'S FIERCELY INDEPENDENT FREEDOM OF INQUIRY

FOR TAN, AIER WAS a breath of fresh air. In summer 2007 she arrived armed with data collected on temperatures in central England from the mid-16th century to end of 20th century. She set to analyzing the figures for a paper examining whether there was local warming during the British Industrial Revolution — a topic relating to the current debate on global warming. "The idea is if industrialization increased temperatures, we ought to see a distinct difference in the temperatures between the pre-industrial and post-industrial periods," she explained. " I'm trying to examine whether, statistically speaking, there was what statisticians call a structural break."

Tan also took time that summer to give a seminar presentation on Hong Kong, where she'd spent a semester in 2006. She discussed whether Hong Kong remained economically free after China took over governance from the United Kingdom in 1997. Her conclusion: "Hong Kong isn't as free as a lot of people presume after the handover. The Chinese government has restructured the legal practices, and is imposing civil law rather than common law. It also has replaced a fully elected legislature, and imposed one in which 50 percent of the seats are selected among business interests that are pro-Beijing.

"I was rather pessimistic about Hong Kong. That's contrary to what a lot of people think. The Heritage Foundation has repeatedly ranked Hong Kong as the No. 1 freest economy in the world. That's true, but it isn't as free as it used to be. I'm comparing it across time, rather than across countries."

Forming a contrary view was acceptable at AIER — just as long as the facts supported it. Tan intended to apply for yet another research fellowship. "I hope they want me back," she said.

OBITUARY FOR HELEN HARWOOD, IN THE BERKSHIRE EAGLE, FEB. 18, 1999

CHAPTER 7

Helen Longfellow Fowle Harwood, 93, of Casa Dorinda, Montecito, California, died February 15 of pneumonia following a 1995 stroke. Born in West Lebanon, New Hampshire, she was one of the first women sports reporters for the *Boston Globe* from 1928-1930. Registrar for the Engineering Economics Foundation, Boston, from 1930-1932, and Secretary of the Corporation to the American Institute for Economic Research of Great Barrington from 1934-1964. She also was an AIER Incorporator and life-time Voting Member of the Corporation.

She married Col. Edward C. Harwood, founder and former Director of AIER, October 1938 in Portsmouth, New Hampshire. She critiqued and helped edit many AIER publications and authored *How to Balance Your Budget*. She was an avid bridge player, was active in local scouting, and helped to arrange the first formal ballroom dancing classes for boys and girls in Great Barrington.

In addition to her sister Lucy E. Ruiter of Brunswick, Maine, she leaves her son William F. Harwood and his wife Diana Piatkowski Harwood; her daughter Eve C. Harwood of New York; her son Frederick C. Harwood and his wife Michelle Linder Harwood; and her daughter Katherine S. Delay and her husband Christian of Marina Del Rey, California. She also leaves two step-children, Marjorie Greer and her husband James of Nottingham, New Hampshire; and Edward T. Harwood of Exeter, New Hampshire. In addition to five grandchildren and eight step-grandchildren, she leaves eight great-grandchildren and 17 great step-grandchildren.

She has made an anatomical gift of her remains to the University of Southern California School of Medicine. A family memorial will be held in Great Barrington later this year. Those who wish to may make donations in her name to their favorite charity.

1) Anna Schwartz, economist at the National Bureau of Economic Research, and who collaborated with Milton Friedman on *A Monetary History of the United States*, provides her perspective on the Euro during a 2005 summer seminar. 2) Walker Todd, frequent visiting research fellow, drops a lobster into the pot for the Institute's traditional summertime lobster feed. 3) A volleyball net set on the lawn behind the Castle is a popular site for summer students to grab fresh air at the end of the day. 4) Students wind down after a long week of research and study at one of the homey restaurants in Great Barrington. 5) Students absorb a fellowship orientation, summer 2007. 6) Student fellows say goodbye at the end of their four-week term, summer 2007.

1) Attendees of the 2004 Property Rights Conference at AIER included, from left, Bruce Godfrey, Utah State faculty member and national expert on the economics of using public and private lands; author and Constitutional scholar Eugene Schroder; Russell Grider, president of the Institute for Consumer and Rural Studies; and Michael Nivison, a village administrator from Cloudcroft, New Mexico. 2) Geoff Hodgson, head of the Centre for Research in Institutional Economics in Great Britain, and editor-in-chief of the *Journal of Institutional Economics*, delivers a PowerPoint presentation at AIER in March 2007. Flanking him is the image of American economist and social critic Thorstein Veblen, cofounder of the Institutional Economics movement. 3) Anna Schwartz checks on the price of the Euro in the *Wall Street Journal*. 4) AIER staff set up lights and a video camera in the conference room before a lecture at a March 2007 conference. Tapes of lectures are archived at AIER. 5) Attendees filled the auditorium during a March 2007 conference lecture.

CHAPTER 7

1) C. Lowell Harriss (left), AIER trustee, emeritus professor of economics at Columbia and former economic consultant to the U.S. treasurer and to the United Nations, was a speaker at the institute's summer 2006 session. At right is Michael Rizzo, senior economist at AIER and director of the summer fellowship program. 2) AIER president and CEO Charles Murray visits with guest lecturer Dominic Salvatore, distinguished professor of economics at Fordham University, during a summer 2007 session on globalization and world governance. 3) Economist Ernest Welker speaks with Nobel Prize-winning physiologist Gerald Edelman during a break in a 2003 conference of the Behavioral Research Institute. 4) Dr. Gerald Edelman — who won the 1972 Nobel Prize for physiology or medicine — speaks at a summer 2003 conference of the Behavioral Research Institute at AIER. The conference topic was, "Dewey, Hayek and Embodied Cognition Experience, Beliefs and Rules." Flanking Edelman is a portrait of Friedrich Hayek, Austrian-born economist and pioneer in political theory and psychology. 5) Vernon Smith, who shared the Nobel Prize in Economics in 2002, addresses a 2003 summer conference of the Behavioral Research Institute. At far left is Wake Forest professor John H. Wood, visiting research fellow, author and expert on macroeconomic policy.

CHAPTER EIGHT
THE 2000S:
NEW MILLENNIUM WITH OLD PROBLEMS;
AIER REACHES NEW MARKETS

A double whammy struck the U.S. economy in the first two years of the new millennium, reversing the exuberance of the 1990s. On March 10, 2000, the NASDAQ index, full of high-tech companies, peaked — marking the fullest expansion of the speculative dot-com bubble that had begun swelling five years before. But investors were taking note of the "burn rate" — the exhaustion of capital gained from venture capitalists and initial public offerings — of these nonviable startups that sought to grow their customer base rather than their bottom line. Annual and quarterly reports released that month showed dismal performance by Internet retailers following the previous Christmas season — underscoring the flaw in these companies' growth-over-profit model. By 2001, most dot-coms had quit trading, and they'd earned the moniker "dot-bombs." The overheated economy was fast cooling.

On Sept. 11, 2001, 19 Al-Qaeda-affiliated terrorists hijacked four U.S. commercial airliners, crashing them individually into the twin World Trade Center towers in New York City and the Pentagon in Arlington, Virginia. A fourth, presumably on its way to Washington, D.C., crashed into a Pennsylvania field. Nearly

3,000 innocent people, in addition to the hijackers, were killed. In the aftermath, President George W. Bush's "War on Terror" resulted in an invasion of Afghanistan and toppling of the Al Qaeda-supporting Taliban regime, and in 2003, an invasion and occupation of Iraq.

Sept. 17, 2001 — the first day of trading after the 9-11 attacks —witnessed the largest

Smoke billows from atop the World Trade Center towers on Sept. 11, 2001, in New York City.

one-day point drop in the century-plus history of the Dow Jones Industrial Average: 684.81 points (7.1 percent). But fueled by the war effort and other factors, such as low interest rates that spawned an enormous housing boom — the Dow reached new peaks by early 2006, including closing above 12,000 for the first time (coincidentally), on the 19th anniversary of "Black Monday" — Oct. 19, 1987. Yet the market continued on a dizzying roller-coaster ride. It swung 1 or more than 2 percent in a single session, rocked by turbulent economic events, from the soaring value of foreign currency versus the U.S. dollar, to Federal Reserve cuts in interest rates, and shakiness in the U.S. sub-prime mortgage market (the field that had, in part, driven the housing boom, and resulted in massive foreclosures). The Dow set a record closing high of 14,164.53 on Oct. 9, 2007, yet four months later had fallen nearly 2,000 points.

The Dow's volatility characterized the strange first decade of the new century, when events proved difficult to interpret. Enron, among the world's leading providers of electricity and natural gas, pulp and paper, had been named "America's Most Innovative Company" six years running by Fortune Magazine. In

Wall Street experienced massive market swings in the 2000s, as consumers and home-buyers piled up debt, and the dollar plunged.

2000, Enron claimed $111 billion in revenues. By the end of the following year, Enron claimed bankruptcy, as the public learned Enron's reported financial state had been based on fraudulent accounting.

Where did the nation's economy stand as the first decade of the new century drew to a close? Major concerns stood out. America, observers could say, had become a country of debtors.

The Social Security system, in terms of dollars paid (nearly $500 billion in benefits in 2004), represented the largest government program in the world and the single biggest expense for taxpayers. Members of the demographic bulge known as the baby boom were increasingly entering retirement age and claiming their benefits. Social Security took up 20.9 percent, and Medicare 20.4 percent, of the federal budget, respectively. Moreover, Social Security was a $12 trillion unfunded liability, and Medicare a $30 trillion unfunded liability.

Gross U.S. external debt (owed to foreign creditors) was about $12 trillion. National debt (owed by government) was about $9 trillion, as was corporate debt. Mortgage debt was

> 66We have a pretty good record of forecasting recessions. Generally, forecasters tend to be reluctant to say a recession is coming. If you work for a big financial firm and want people to think that things are good, that it's a good time to invest or to take out a loan, the forecasters who work for them are often under pressure to say there's not a recession coming.99
>
> — *Kerry Lynch, AIER director of education and research*

more than $10 trillion. In 2006, the U.S. economy showed its lowest saving rate since 1933, in the depths of the Great Depression.

In 2008, that strange economic beast known as stagflation — a mutant created by rising costs and slowing growth — which had emerged in the 1970s, seemed to be back.

THE INSTITUTE IMPROVES INFRASTRUCTURE, BUILDS FOR NEW MARKETS

AS AIER REACHED ITS 75th year, it continued to improve its infrastructure. In 2002, the E.C. Harwood Library was remodeled, at a cost of $2.5 million, and its 20,000 square feet on two stories now housed offices (where a parking garage had been), classrooms, a multifunction lecture hall, and a 100-seat auditorium to host acclaimed critical thinkers dedicated to advancing economic and behavioral knowledge. Indeed, the

Institute's abiding mission seemed as relevant as ever. It mailed monthly *Economic Education Bulletins* and twice-monthly *Research Reports* to 11,000 sustaining members. Its sales of books numbered about 200,000 a year, ranking AIER among the largest providers of private economic education in the nation.

In 2006, the Institute commissioned a study by the Zone 5 market-research firm, based in Albany, New York, to identify the Institute's strengths and weaknesses vis-à-vis the needs of current AIER subscribers and book buyers, and to provide direction on growing the Institute's audience. Among the findings were that AIER subscribers and book buyers shared similar demographics. Customers were predominantly over 40 years of age; about 15 percent were over 80; just over 25 percent ages 70-79; about 23 percent 60-69; 20 percent 50-59; about 12 percent 40-49; about 4 percent 30-39; and about 1 percent 20-29.

CHAPTER 8

> 66One of the things we can be proudest of here is that people value our work. Eleven thousand subscribers are paying $59 a year for our publications. Most places like us have to give it away.99
>
> — *Lawrence Pratt, AIER senior fellow, and developer of the High Yield Dow system used by AIS.*

A thumbnail sketch of a "typical" AIER customer was a person over 43 years old, likely to be retired and with no children living at home, owning a single-family home, not particularly affluent compared to fellow Americans (only 23 percent commanded a personal income above $100,000), and not concerned about social status or prestige.

Highlights of the study's findings included that "AIER is an important, relevant institution that offers a broad set of financial education products for every stage in life," and that the products "are credible, relevant and important," and an "excellent value" based on a price-content comparison. AIER, however, suffered from low awareness and a weak brand — meaning there was ample opportunity to increase the Institute's marketing. What's more, Zone 5's research showed "an inverse relationship between the need for financial information and the desire to seek it." Fertile new customer bases for AIER to

pursue included people in the 35-45 age range; individuals and families with low to moderate incomes with less experience than traditional AIER customers with complicated financial transaction, such as buying a home, and who may be more susceptible to financial deception and fraud; and immigrants needing information on living within the U.S. economic system.

Another study recommendation was to provide products beyond the Institute's printed products written at the college level. New products could be adapted to formats more palatable for new customer bases, such as online subscriptions, demonstrative videos, and emailed material.

The study concluded: "With minor changes to the products, extension into electronic delivery, and the implementation of a strategic marketing program, AIER should enjoy significant growth for years to come." ❖

ROBERT GILMOUR:
PARTING OBSERVATIONS FROM AN OUTGOING PRESIDENT

The 12 years — 1991 to 2003 — that Robert A. Gilmour served as president and CEO of the American Institute for Economic Research spanned a transitional period when the organization recovered from financial and organizational challenges to emerge stronger than ever.

Gilmour's involvement with AIER began in 1983, when he came aboard as a senior analyst after earning his doctorate from Johns Hopkins and serving on the faculties of Princeton and Michigan, among

Robert Gilmour served as president and CEO of AIER from 1991 to 2003.

other universities. Before taking the helm as AIER's president, Gilmour served as director of research and education 1985-91. Today he is president emeritus.

The following article ran in the Dec. 23, 2002, issue of *Research Reports*, and represents Gilmour's parting observations, summations and conjectures about the Institute from which he would retire at year's end.

THE FAT LADY SINGS

Life doesn't owe you a living. So my parents said and so I believe. Dad was blunt: If you don't work, you don't eat. Mom pushed it further: You can be anything you want to be if you work hard enough. That world, where parents without fear of reprisal told their kids what was right and what was wrong, how to get along in life by excelling, and what to expect (sometimes very negatively) from their fellows, is the world in which I was raised.

For mom and dad, life held great uncertainty. I probably would not have been born had it not been for the stock-market crash in 1929. Dad rode shotgun on a truck for Crown Zellerbach. Mom was a career woman with money in stocks. Dad said they shouldn't marry until he was the main support of the family, regardless of her wealth. You can guess what happened: Mom was wiped out in the crash, put the question to him (he was worth just as much as she after the crash), and on Nov. 2, 1929, they married. I was one of the results.

My early childhood, as that of my brother and many others, was informed by depression, war, loss, fear, and incalculable uncertainty about the future in all ways. It didn't help that, by the mid-1950s, nuclear war seemed impending. But we managed — and prospered.

THE UNCERTAINTY PERPLEX

This is not to say that my parents or my contemporaries faced especially uncertain times and by extraordinary virtue somehow triumphed. Anyone with a sense of history or place ought to be cautious about naming a "greatest generation." Today, billions live in circumstances that, by comparison, make *any* American generation appear comfortably secure. Rather, the point is that life is uncertain no matter what the circumstances of one's birth (and has only one outcome). An overriding concern for all generations at any time and any place would seem to have been how to reduce such uncertainty. In one way or another, *that* concern always has been central to this Institute's work.

It should not, however, be confused with what John Dewey termed the human "Quest for Certainty." Indeed, while there can be no such thing as a coda for a work in progress, as the title of this piece might imply, a fundamental mission of the American Institute for Economic Research has been to illuminate the hazards of the pursuit of "absolute truth," "final solutions," or any of the other notions that in our view have impeded human progress over the centuries from the Dark Ages to Nazi Germany to the "scientific socialism" of late. Today that quest seems to have acquired many forms.

To those buoyant adherents of the belief in inevitable human progress through advances in science and technology, who dominated much of American progressive thought from the early decades of the 20th century through the postwar era and beyond, current events almost surely would be unsettling. Despite the worldwide reverses that socialist notions have encountered in recent decades — which is a very good thing indeed — that impending global religious conflict would now pose the most imminent threat to the survival of human civilization probably was unthinkable. Although many factors are involved, as I described in "The Aftermath" (*Research Reports*, Sept. 24, 2001), the currents that now threaten us all seem linked at bottom to the Quest for Certainty, which often seems manifest in resistance to change — any type of which promotes uncertainty. It scarcely needs noting that change seems a most reliable feature of life, and as such virtually guarantees that the quest will persist.

Whether the world as we know it might disintegrate quickly in the wake of global catastrophe or erode slowly under the corrosive effects of persistent terrorism — or what circumstances the survivors might encounter — no one knows. Nor is it easy to say whether the risks of today are lesser or greater than they were, say, 40 years ago when the civilized world was poised on the brink of nuclear holocaust during the Cuban missile crisis. Or centuries ago when famine and misery and early death were statistical probabilities.

Again, the point is that every generation confronts its own uncertainties. Science and technology, while they may and do have great beneficial effects in raising standards of living, do not necessarily imply greater certainty with respect to the characteristics of human transaction or to enduring fears promoted by change. On the contrary, many today apparently believe that science and technology have fostered unprecedented uncertainty in all walks of life — even to the extent that fundamental natural processes are imperiled and all life on the planet endangered.

In this view, by introducing the further complications involved with multicultural transaction, "globalization" has simply compounded the perceived problems — and so has been demonized by a variety of interest groups whose only shared characteristic is preserving the status quo. In short, the quest for certainty seems likely to continue to be as central to human behavior today as it has throughout recorded history.

A NEW TWIST IN THE PERSISTENCE OF FANTASY

But it may have taken an unexpected twist. In previous eras the confrontation between "science" and "art" (both of which in different ways may be engaged in the quest for certainty) has been pretty clearly drawn. It was succinctly described by C.P. Snow in his classic work *The Two Cultures* (which, incidentally, was a strong influence on my decision to pursue behavioral science and which I still highly recommend). Today, however, the barrier between science and art as described by Snow and others in one sense would seem to have been breached — and not necessarily with favorable implications for the resolution of human problems stemming from the quest for certainty.

To a seemingly unprecedented extent technological innovation in recent years in the most advanced economies has promoted rather than resisted the retreat to fantasy that has been a persistent characteristic of the quest for certainty throughout the ages. I am referring, of course, to the computer revolution, the implications of whose binary transaction may be more far-reaching than most would credit.

Very simply, today many of the most talented young people across the globe inhabit a world where successful transaction (emphatically not human transaction in a conventional sense) is guaranteed if the rules of binary science are met. This virtual world — a euphemism for fantasy world — could turn out to be more influential than one might hope. Given the exploding market for its products (such as ever more "realistic" video games), its potential transcends even the most radical predictions of early media-age gurus such as Marshall ("The medium is the message") McLuhan. The economic rewards for the pursuit of fantasy are as great today as they ever have been.

THE REJECTION OF USEFUL KNOWLEDGE

Space here does not permit even partial consideration of many of the other myriad manifestations of the uncertainty perplex: Even casual reflection suggests that responses to uncertainty inform a great deal of human behavior. Permit me, then, to focus briefly on one that in my view is most perverse: namely, the postmodernist rejection of useful knowledge.

That even the most accomplished inquiry may not yield final results apparently has troubled many bright people for a long time. It is only in recent years, however, that some of those engaged in the academic disciplines have concluded that, absent absolute truth (i.e., certainty of the outcomes of their efforts) all results are equally valid or invalid. Such notions have spawned a mindless relativism that, as we have noted elsewhere in these *Reports*, in many curricula has rendered a useful understanding of, say, history (it's all bunk), mathematics (any answer will serve if you're glib enough), or even language (make up your own) nearly impossible.

Over the years, it has been a source of considerable dismay that our readers sometimes have confused our epistemological rejection of certainty with this wanton abandonment of useful knowledge. The warranted assertability that we pursue is in fact an emphatic endorsement of the application of useful knowledge to human problems. Even in the absence of certain outcomes, humans are required to act — and in most circumstances some choices are better than others. Although we do not view our results as final in any sense, they provide a basis for informed action, and, as the example below may suggest, may be highly beneficial.

CHARLES MURRAY: PRESIDENT AND CEO EXPANDS AIER'S OUTREACH TO SCHOLARS AND SUBSCRIBERS

Since taking over as president and chief executive officer of the American Institute for Economic Research in 2003, Charles Murray has pursued goals of raising awareness about AIER's work among economists, increasing the number and quality of visiting speakers and scholars, and developing new products — in line with the Institute's original mission set in 1933 — to help the average citizen protect his or her assets.

As a result, by 2007 the number of annual sustaining members surpassed 11,000 —

President and CEO Charles Murray.

approaching the Institute's record. Sales of AIER books continued to average about 200,000 a year, ranking the Institute among the largest providers of private economic education in the nation. The market value of assets held in the Institute's charitable remainder unitrusts exceeded $150 million. And a well-developed Internet presence, coupled with plans for reaching new audiences identified by a marketing study, boded well for expanding the Institute's products and readership.

Meanwhile, AIER was drawing more visitors than ever to its headquarters in Great Barrington. AIER was holding one or two academic conferences a year, beckoning economists with stellar pedigrees as well as those on the field's fringe. The Institute also had divided its eight-week summer fellowship period into two four-week sessions, while courting top researchers, guest speakers and collegiate scholars. These moves were lifting AIER's profile.

"In general, just as AIER brings in more people to study and research and speak at our Institute, and they leave and tell their friends about us, we're becoming more known," Murray said. "In recent years we've tended to bring in more and better students and visiting scholars. We have, of course, enjoyed distinguished students and scholars in years past, and many are still associated with us. We've been fairly successful in making inroads among the public who reads our publications, who call them useful. For a while, we were somewhat insular and not necessarily recognized among the academic community and researchers. We want to make sure we're known among our peers for doing quality work."

Sheer objective, scientifically valid research, uncompromised by special interests, has been the Institute's hallmark from its inception. "We've always gone for quality, and not necessarily notoriety," Murray said. "AIER will never be a household name. That's not our goal. Other think tanks, such as the Cato Institute or the Heritage Foundation, are funded by special interests. To get bigger, a lot of other groups take grants and other donations, and there are always strings attached. Our whole aim is having no strings attached; therefore we can do what we want to do. We can stick our thumb in anybody's eye. If we ever lost that independence, we wouldn't be unique, and there'd be no reason for us to exist.

CHAPTER 8

"Our goal is to provide useful, noncommercial, non-governmental information to people. That's what we excel at."

INSTITUTE'S DEEP ANALYSIS PROVES REFRESHING

MURRAY HIMSELF WAS WELL along in his career as an economist before he learned of AIER's existence. The field of economics itself was a mystery to him before he entered college. He was raised in the Poconos in northeastern Pennsylvania, where his father owned a hardware store in the small town of Honesdale, surrounded by dairy farms. "I grew up in an area that was very rural and agriculture based," Murray said. "Therefore I had no concept of really studying what happens to the economy, because our little part of the world was insulated from markets."

But when he attended Shippensburg University, in south-central Pennsylvania, pursuing a bachelor's degree in business administration, his economics courses and professors fascinated him. "Studying economics opened new horizons to things I had no clue about," he said. Murray earned a doctorate in economics from Iowa State University, with special interests in monetary theory, the history of thought, and financial economics. He was an assistant professor of economics at Truman State University in Kirksville, Missouri, when he attended an American Economics Association conference in New Orleans in 1997. There he met AIER staffers Kerry Lynch and Lawrence Pratt and president Robert Gilmour. Murray began reading the Institute's publications. He was favorably impressed.

"I liked that the Institute wrote materials for the layman, but they still were fairly sophisticated," he said. "The other thing was that AIER researchers took points of view that most academic economists or business economists never take — and the views were supported by data and research."

Murray found that AIER's research and analysis ran deeper than works characteristic of college faculty. "A lot of economic theory deals with market failure, and most academic economists spend their lives focusing on market failure, and then move toward using economic theory and tools to fix that. What a lot of them don't realize is that governments trying to fix market failure can fail, too. You're showing me on the blackboard that markets fail, and assume there's some fix for it, but never follow through and analyze whether the fix works. But such analysis is one of the things AIER does. We look at all the implications."

AIER researchers also take a long-range perspective on issues. "If you look at any of our charts, they go back as far as you can get the data," Murray said. "We take a historical look at things. And we tend to take a long-run view going the other way. If we analyze whether fiat currency has ever held its value, we're not checking whether it will lose its value tomorrow. We look out over decades and centuries, to what's happened historically. Or if you want to know how the gold standard worked, or would work, you might look at past episodes of what happened. I don't think you can perfectly project into the future and say the future will be like the past. But the past does give you information."

SCRUPULOUSLY INDEPENDENT AIER ATTRACTS 'FREE THINKERS'

MURRAY JOINED AIER IN 1998 as a senior economist and as director of fellowship programs. He became the director of research and education in 2000, and president and CEO on Jan.1, 2003. He proudly touts the Institute's standards for utter scientific objectivity — one of the reasons AIER draws ruggedly independent scholars who thrive in its environment.

"We're more than a free-market think tank," Murray said. "We're free thinkers. People at the Heritage Foundation aren't free to express what's on their mind. People at the Federal Reserve aren't free to express what's on their mind. That's how we get all their 'rejects.' Walker Todd, one of our fellowship program instructors and a research fellow, worked at the Federal Reserve Bank of Cleveland, and said what was on his mind, and they said, 'You're not going to be here.' As far as academic economists, the reality is they don't always have the ability to say what they want to say. These economists write grants to fund studies. If somebody does a labor study funded by labor unions, how independent is that? It's a Faustian pact."

AIER's commitment to intellectual freedom includes inviting visiting scholars whose stances diverge greatly. "We're not just tied to our views and fellow travelers'," Murray said. "We bring in people from a wide range of the economic and political spectrum. For example, Thomas Naylor, head of the secession movement in Vermont. We've had Marxists here. This is one of the few places they can go and express their views openly. It's not that they won't be questioned. But they won't be censored. They'll get raked over the coals, as is everybody, in the questioning period after their presentations. But their views are able to be expressed."

Murray sees irony in that some of AIER's longtime views on the economy finally have become mainstream. That is, the mainstream is shifting to AIER's positions. "We were talking about free markets years ago, and they were foreign ideas to the mainstream, where the idea was the government can fix everything. AIER hasn't caused the reversal, but it's been part of the reason markets are more accepted, and people are starting to question programs we've criticized. We're not a Johnny-come-lately to saying Social Security wouldn't work. We said it wouldn't work before it existed."

AIER's role throughout its three-quarters of a century in existence has been to provide

CHAPTER 8

practical financial information to the individual citizen, whom founder E.C. Harwood termed "the industrious and thrifty, those who pay most of the nation's taxes," and "are the principal guardians of American civilization." "We believe in individual sovereignty," Murray said. "Let productive people be. We produce research and publish information to help the people protect what they have."

Toward that end, the Institute continues to consider new means of making its publications available — such as putting versions on the Institute's website, and placing books in mainstream bookstores, and on college campuses as supplemental readers to textbooks. Meanwhile, books geared to newer audiences and addressing subjects of widespread interest are being contemplated. These, Murray said, could include a financial survival guide for young people heading off to college, and who will need to know how to handle apartment leases, student loans and credit cards. Another title could cover the basic economics of getting divorced.

In every instance, book content would be based on good, solid, useful information collected through independent, unbiased research — AIER's signature approach.

AIER remains an anomaly among think tanks, a nonprofit organization whose bylaws prohibit accepting gifts from private foundations, commercial interests or the government. The Institute survives from its sales of newsletters and books, and from support from donors who respect the importance of an independent economic perspective.

"Any economist will say that what we're trying to do will not work," Murray said. "But we've got the contrapositive. We're here, and we're thriving. That's so characteristic of AIER. The evidence is contrary to what the theory would tell you."

KERRY LYNCH: DIRECTOR OF RESEARCH AND EDUCATION IS PROUD OF AIER'S FORECASTING RECORD

When Kerry Lynch signed a six-month contract in 1987 with the American Institute for Economic Research to write a book on retirement planning, she couldn't have foreseen that she'd end up a permanent staff member, much less the Institute's director of research education. "I was not familiar with the place until I started working here," said Lynch, who'd earned her bachelor's in economics from Bryn Mawr College and her master's from Duke University. That training, plus her skill at writing, led her to the book assignment at AIER.

Once at AIER, she began reading the Institute's books and *Research Reports*. The more she read, the more she was impressed. "It was a take on the economy and economic issues that I hadn't seen in graduate school, or as an undergraduate," she said. "The views were very thoughtfully presented, and very persuasive and reasonably presented."

Lynch stayed on at the Institute, progressing to assistant director of research and education, then associate director, and finally, in 2004, director. Along the way, she penned a large number of articles for the Institute's *Research Reports* and

Director of Research and Education Kerry Lynch.

Economic Education Bulletins on topics ranging from fiscal policy to monetary policy, Social Security, Medicare, and retirement planning. As an AIER faculty member, she's taught a seminar on business-cycle analysis for the Summer Fellowship program.

LONG-HELD VIEWS PROVE TO BE ON THE CUTTING EDGE

AIER'S VIEWS ON THE economy haven't fundamentally changed since the days when founder E.C. Harwood was first touting free-market principles and assailing federal economic policies. But the Institute's research-based take on contemporary issues has remained ahead of the curve. That's a source of pride for Lynch. Take Social Security. In the 1930s, when President Roosevelt's administration created the Social Security system, Harwood cautioned that the current generation was "attempting to provide for *our own* old age at the expense of our children and grandchildren."

"He was warning that it would not be the panacea that many people thought it was," Lynch said. "It would eventually run into problems, and it has. We've been looking at the trust funds since they were created in the 1980s, and pointing out that they're an accounting device, not really a pool of money to draw on. We don't take the view that the whole system will collapse or go bankrupt. But there's definitely going to be financing issues, particularly as the baby boomers are retiring. And that's been evident for a long time. Eventually something will have to give. The government will have to borrow more, or it may trim benefits. Objectively, you can look at the demographics and say there's going to be a problem. It would have been better to deal with it earlier, when the baby boomers were younger, rather than wait until they're ready to retire."

AIER researchers were warning about an impending savings and loan crisis well before it materialized in the late 1980s. And in July 2007, the Institute was forecasting the recession that mainstream media finally reported in February 2008. AIER's special tools — a historically established set of Leading, Lagging and Coincident economic indicators; and a separate mathematical analysis that yields a cyclical score — allow its researchers to objectively assess the phase of the business cycle.

"We have a pretty good record of forecasting recessions," Lynch said. "Generally, forecasters don't have a very good record with that, and tend to be reluctant to say a recession is coming. A lot of business analysts work for companies that have an interest in saying that things are good. If you work for a big financial firm and want people to think that things are good, that it's a good time to invest or to take out a loan, the forecasters who work for them are often under pressure to say there's not a recession coming."

In summer 2007, most of the 12 Leading Indicators, including the housing market, were trending downward — characteristic of an impending contraction in the economy. But AIER analysts refrained from predicting how long the recession would last. All they do is look at the data to see where the economy is. And that information is disseminated to anyone who cares to listen.

"Our audience has mainly been the public," Lynch said. "We've reached many, many thousands of people who have bought our publications or subscribed to them over the years. That's been our target: the ordinary American, not policy makers or government. It's a noble mission to try to educate the general public. We try very hard to do that."

LAWRENCE PRATT: SOLITARY RESEARCHER, THRIVES IN AIER'S RARE ENVIRONMENT

Lawrence Pratt's route to the American Institute for Economic Research led first to the subtropical farmlands of Malawi in southeastern Africa, then to the marble halls of commerce in New York City. The real-world lessons in economics he absorbed supplemented the bachelor's degree he earned from Yale.

First as a Peace Corps volunteer in Malawi, then as a government employee, Pratt helped operate a system called "bush marketing." A government agency, combating underpayment by buyers, set a market price and attempted to ensure that peasant farmers got fairly compensated

Senior fellow Larry Pratt, who's also served as AIER director of research and education, and as president of American Investment Services.

for their crops of tobacco and cotton, peanuts and other produce. A worker would be dispatched with gunnysacks and a box of money to visit the farmers. He'd come back two weeks later and hope to find the gunnysacks full of crops and the money gone.

Pratt's next job dealt with a far more sophisticated sector of finance: He was a bond analyst for the New York Life Insurance Company. In 1973 he moved to the Great Barrington area, where he'd grown up and owned a family house. He took a job as a staff economist at the American Institute for Economic Research, attracted by its philosophy. "It did not have a terribly dogmatic view of the conventional economics that I was taught," Pratt said.

A self-motivated researcher who thrives in the solitude necessary to produce in-depth analysis, Pratt proved to be highly productive in AIER's scholarly environment, and has remained at the Institute ever since. He's written hundreds of articles for Institute publications, and served in posts ranging from director of research and education, to president of the Institute's affiliate, American Investment Services. He is proud that its investment counseling and management differ from that of the typical investment firm. "Its mission, historically, is less oriented toward gouging the customer than serving the customer as best we could," Pratt said. "Our fees are much less than most other advisers."

DEVELOPING THE 'HYD,' AND A MODEL FOR ASSESSING THE BUSINESS CYCLE

PRATT'S INTENSIVE STUDIES OF the market have shaped AIS's investment strategies. One feature is the "High Yield Dow." Pratt created a database showing the performances of the 30 stocks in the Dow Jones Industrial Average over different holding periods. He determined that if an investor consistently purchased, every month, the top four stocks with the highest yields, and held them for 18 months, the investor would wind up with a portfolio with the best combination of return and risk.

CHAPTER 8

Pratt's best-known contribution at AIER has been his development of a mathematical model for assessing the business cycle. AIER researchers had been analyzing the Leading, Lagging and Coincident economic indicators since they were first published in the 1950s by the National Bureau of Economic Research. AIER added a new mechanism for analyzing business cycles, "the Diffusion Index," which shows the percent of each indicator expanding cyclically.

The AIER staff meets once a month to appraise the status of each indicator and make a judgment on where the economy stands in the business cycle. But the element of human bias cannot be removed. To modulate potential inaccuracy from that factor, Pratt developed a mathematical model to give a Cyclical Score to each series of indicators. If a series goes down for 11 months, it shows the economy is contracting. If it goes up for 11 months, it's clearly expanding. In between, the staff looks at reversals in the trend. The Cyclical Scores are an attempt to eliminate the fudge factor and false signals.

At present, Pratt is a senior fellow at AIER, and is happy to have spent nearly his entire career at the Institute. "The specialness of this place is that you're pretty much on your own," he said. As a researcher and writer, one is free to come up with analysis of issues — as long as one can back it up with hard data and reasoning.

"One of the things we can be proudest of here is that people value our work," Pratt said. "Eleven thousand subscribers are paying $59 a year for our publications. Most places like us have to give it away."

BRUCE GORE: THE MAN WHO KEEPS THE FACILITIES RUNNING, THE GROUNDS GROOMED AND NAVIGABLE

The campus of the American Institute for Economic Research encompasses approximately 110 acres of bucolic woods and pastures, hills and streams teeming with plants and wildlife. While the buildings and primary section of the campus are in Great Barrington, the property straddles the line between the townships of Great Barrington and Alford, with 25 acres of wooded land falling within the latter's realm.

AIER hums with activity year-round, through winter's heavy snows and spring's torrents, summer's swelter and fall's cascade of leaves. The vital tasks of overseeing the aging and modern facilities and surrounding grounds falls on the shoulders of Bruce Gore — a man with a long relationship with the Institute. Gore, AIER's facilities manager, supervises the combined effort of a limited staff and of a group of outsourced contractors in the areas of grounds maintenance, heating, ventilation and air-conditioning, plumbing, electrical, security, and cleaning services. The myriad responsibilities range from ensuring the proper operation of the steam boiler in the seven-decade-old "Castle," to managing the computerized HVAC system of the library, a small public water-supply system, a private waste-disposal system, and day-to-day emergencies. Apart from overseeing the buildings and infrastructure at the campus's core, Gore supervises the upkeep of the 15 acres of surrounding meadowland, seeing that they are mowed and trimmed amid the wild fields and forests of maples and oak, ash and pine.

Bruce Gore, manager of facilities, also directed AIER's printing plant before its closure in 2007. Gore has filled numerous positions at the Institute for three decades.

Then there is the matter of access to campus. Someone has to ensure that the winding, mile-long road leading from the stone gate on Division Street through the woods to the Library, Castle and Annex is kept clear during the snowy New England winters.

That man is Bruce Gore — who is intimately familiar with every inch of the buildings and every mile of the natural location.

A LOYAL EMPLOYEE AND HAPPY RESIDENT OF THE INSTITUTE

GORE'S PATH TO AIER hardly was direct. After growing up in nearby Lenox and graduating high school, he took what he expected would be a part-time job at AIER in fall 1973 as a driver and handyman. While he was attending evening classes at a community college with the expectation of enrolling full time down the road, a job opening arose in AIER's pressroom, which Gore accepted and where he learned the folding and darkroom operations. A couple of years later, he took over after the pressman left, and in time rose to supervisor of the printing and mailing section. Little by little, Gore assumed management of the buildings and grounds, working under Col. E.C. Harwood's son Fred.

For seven years, beginning in 1974 until he was married, Gore lived in the Castle. That afforded him contact with Col. Harwood, who also resided in the Castle when he spent time in Great Barrington. The Colonel ended up having a large influence on the young man. As Gore recalls: "When I first met him, he was wearing Army fatigues and appeared rather crisp. He walked with a purpose and with an air of authority. In time he turned out to be a pretty decent chap, showed a sense of humor, and was appreciative of those who worked diligently for AIER's purposes.

"Even in his retirement he had his finger on the pulse of the business. He would walk through the printing and mailing section, sometimes ask a question, and look at a press sheet or what was being inserted and mailed on one of the machines. He could remember a great deal and was very good with logistics. He had the ability to analyze people through conversation, understand their skill set, and what their capacity for learning was. It took awhile, but with time I began to know him a bit and eventually hit it off with him and his wife, Helen, quite well. I understood the mission after a few years and jumped on board rather than going to school. I said, 'This is for me, I like it here.'"

The intellectual atmosphere nurtured Gore's budding interest in economics and theory. "I would sit up there at lunch or dinner, elbow to elbow with high-powered economists, visiting professors and graduate students, soaking up commentary on economic issues," he said. Gleaning information from staff, and reading the Institute's publications as well as the *Wall Street Journal*, Gore switched his views from the influence of his father's support of Franklin D. Roosevelt's style of government to that of Col. Harwood's free-market philosophy.

"When Col. Harwood was in residence, the nightly news airings in the TV room were well attended and often turned into an impromptu economics lesson, but without the formality of a classroom," Gore remembered. "From time to time I consumed a crumb or two of knowledge that fell off the plate of the conversation. Those were good times."

RAISING A FAMILY AT AIER

AFTER GORE'S MARRIAGE — to a woman whom he met while making AIER's daily deposit at a local bank — he moved into a company-owned apartment. "The AIER environment was an excellent place to raise small children," he said. "Walks into the surrounding woodlots exposed them to all the delights of nature and helped them develop a healthy respect for nature and wildlife."

In 1988, Gore and his wife bought land and built their own home in Great Barrington for their family of four. In 1996, with some reservation, he left the employment of AIER and began work as a building contractor, building and woodworking being lifelong passions of his. After nine years in the business he returned to AIER in fall 2005 as the production and facilities manager, which included supervising the print shop, in which 9 million documents were produced and shipped each year. Much has changed over the years in the printing and mailing industry, and it was increasingly clear that AIER could not compete with outside printing and mailing contractors in the face of rapid changes in technology and direct-mail advertising. In 2007, the Institute finally closed its in-plant production department, and Gore's duties shifted entirely to managing and planning for the use of facilities and grounds, and occasionally assisting with production issues.

In retrospect, Gore appreciated that he could not have found a more beautiful setting than the AIER campus in which to spend his time in the area of buildings and grounds maintenance. Falls are stunning, with the maples turning yellow, orange, purple or red. Most of the acreage remains fairly wild forests and fields. Waterfowl are abundant: Canada geese, ducks, loons, and occasionally snow geese, great blue herons, egrets, and the like visit the nearby Long Pond. Eastern whitetail deer run heavily on the grounds year round. Black bears have wandered as close to the Castle as the driveway. Bobcats and raccoons roam the woods. An employee aboard a tractor recounted how a coyote followed him around the field he was mowing, pouncing upon any field mice whose grassy cover was being removed.

AIER's seclusion allows for the sort of quiescence amenable to scholars performing the cerebral trade. In addition to students and research fellows during the summer, and conference attendees, the Castle's dormitory-like guest rooms put up overnight visitors, such as American Investment Services clients making a quick stop at the Institute, or a researcher writing an article who needs to meet with the staff. Most guests enjoy their stay in the mansion's archaic but comfortable atmosphere.

What of rumors of ghosts in the Castle? Gore smiled. "I lived in the Main House from 1974 to 1981," he said, "and never had an experience with any ghosts. But I did investigate many initially mysterious sounds that involved a clanking radiator, snow slides off the steep slate roof, or people visiting the building."

JEAN WHITE: THE FIRST SET OF EYES ON INCOMING MAIL

Jean White came to the American Institute for Economic Research in 1961, a Massachusetts native possessed of a New England brogue. After high school she'd moved to Stockbridge, next to Great Barrington, to live with a cousin. After a bookkeeping job at a gas station fell through, White found a position at AIER in the mailroom, and learned from the bottom up, sorting mail, sealing envelopes — and finally taking, in 1969, the position of opening mail. Thirty-eight years later, she still occupied that frontline post in handling

CHAPTER 8

Longtime AIER employee Jean White has the first set of eyes reviewing correspondence to the Institute.

incoming correspondence, working 30 hours a week, 8 a.m. to 3 p.m. with a lunch break.

"I've enjoyed opening the mail," White said. "It's fascinating. No two days are alike with what kind of mail you're going to get, or what kind of horrible stuff people send through the mail. Some are angry letters — 'Take me off your mailing list,' 'Where'd you get my name from?' and so forth. Some people will just tear up the whole circ, put it in the envelope, send it to us with our postage on it, and we have to pay for it. One day I opened up the mail and here's fingernail clippings. I have no idea what that was all about, but I let a scream out. It's strange what people will send through the mail. You don't know."

White sorts and opens the incoming mail. The vast majority of correspondence isn't of the irate or odd variety, though. It's orders or letters from subscribers, or materials from companies with AIER on their mailing lists. One morning she opened four envelopes in a row from the same person, a man in California. One was a membership renewal. Each of the others was a book order. Then White opened a thick envelope. It, too, was from the same man, and contained 12 more book orders. The following morning, she opened another envelope from the same man, with more book orders. He apparently hadn't been able to sustain one clear thought about ordering the books in one single action.

MEMORIES OF SEASONAL STORMS, AND THE CALM COLONEL

WHITE LOVES THE INSTITUTE'S setting, the four seasons. She misses the days before the Edward C. Harwood Library was expanded, when glass windows occupied each outer wall. "I could look out at this beautiful view. You could see the rainstorms and snowstorms coming in the winter. You might see a rainbow. It was just beautiful. I liked the old building. But everything changes."

She definitely missed Col. E.C. Harwood, whom she addressed as "the Colonel." He lived in the Castle, and although he headed the Institute, he always was available for service in the trenches when needed. "I loved him," White said. "He was a very pleasant man. When I first started work up in the mailroom I was working on the inserter, inserting return envelopes. Occasionally during the winter they'd have me come in and work on Saturdays. At different times I did have trouble with the inserter. A couple times I had to go get the Colonel up in his corner office in the main house. He'd come down and work on it."

Not only were his engineering skills adroit, his managerial skills were uncanny. "He could walk through the mailroom," White said, "and if somebody was acting up, he knew it. He would get back to whoever was in charge. He didn't miss anything. Like when I came down to work in the office, opening mail. If we had sent a big mailing out, like circularizing a book, and we weren't getting the book orders the way we should after a week or 10 days, he'd hop in his car and go down to the post office and find out what was going on."

White had full faith in Col. Harwood. Even in the dark days of the U.S. Securities and Exchange Commission, when some trustees and employees worried the Institute would be closed down, White never worried. "Most people figured, knowing the Colonel, things would have to turn out right." They did.

One thing that hasn't changed at AIER is the wildlife on the grounds. "I drove in the other day, this wild turkey is over here on this side of the street," White said. "He sees me coming, what does he do? Crosses the street. I had to slow down for him. Then he gets over here and he stops and looks at me."

Left: Cook Linda Lis ensures staff, fellows and guest speakers remain well-nourished during their stays. Right: Chief financial officer Shaun Buckler.

'A STARBUCKS A DAY PUSHES RETIREMENT AWAY'

The *Research Reports* issue of Aug.6, 2007, featured the article, "A Starbucks a Day Pushes Retirement Away." Its summary: Investing is the glamorous side of personal finance. To be a wise investor, however, it is first necessary to develop and commit to a sensible savings plan — a less glamorous endeavor. Saving is difficult because resources are limited, while opportunities to expend them are unlimited. Nonetheless, even modest frugality today can lay the foundation for increased wealth, and financial independence, in the future.

An excerpt from the article:

Cannot people realize how large an income is thrift? — Cicero

From time to time it is useful to revisit the age-old proverbs that were taught to us as children but have faded from consciousness. Who among us cannot complete the phrase, "a penny saved is . . ."? Yet who pays much attention to its message? That the virtue of thriftiness is espoused in sources as disparate as the Boy Scout Law and Shakespeare's *Hamlet*, by American presidents such as Calvin Coolidge and Teddy Roosevelt, as well as legendary entrepreneurs such as Thomas Edison and John Rockefeller does not render the concept a quaint relic. Rather, it is the mountains of media directing customers to myriad "get rich" investing strategies that have lured many Americans into complacently believing that the way to build personal wealth is to find the appropriate investing tool.

Fortunes rarely fall from the sky or spout from the ground. The key to successful investing is having a source of funds to invest. And while some people may receive sizable bequests or win lotteries, for the vast majority, wealth will come from savings accumulated over the course of their working lives.

It Only Takes a Little

Saving, by definition, entails personal sacrifice — it requires that consumers spend less than they earn. However, the word *sacrifice* connotes something darker than it should in this sense. When individuals save, their foregone consumption is not lost forever; instead it will be recovered many times over in the form of increased future consumption. A surprisingly small sacrifice is required to generate substantial rewards.

How small? About 24 ounces! Take, for example, American coffee consumption. Over 170 million Americans drink coffee, consuming an average of three cups per day. Two "tall" (12 ounce) coffees at Starbucks cost about $6; 24 ounces from a convenience store runs about

$2.25; home brewing costs somewhat less. For the sake of simplicity, assume that the average drinking-on-the-go American spends about $3 a day on coffee.

Suppose that Tom is age 22 and starting his first job out of college. Each day he passes a Starbucks and must decide whether he will stop in and spend $3 on a Triple Grande Latte, or pass by and drink the "free" coffee in his office or at home.

If he chooses to forego the Starbucks, he might invest the $3 in a mutual fund each day, or a total of $1,095 per year. Let's assume the fund earns a real (*i.e.*, inflation adjusted) investment return of 7 percent per year, which is the actual annual real (inflation-adjusted) return achieved by the S&P 500 since 1926.

When Tom saves money, say $1,000 per year, and it earns a return of 7 percent a year, he earns $70 in the first full year of investment. However, at the end of year two, he will earn a return not only on the initial $1,000, but also on the $70, for a total of $74.90 in interest rather than just $70. This is the power of *compound interest*. Each year Tom earns a return not only on the money he saves, but also on the investment earnings accumulated each year.

The effects of compounding are small in the early years. In the above example, Tom earns an additional $4.90 in year two, but the gradually increasing impact of compound interest sets the stage for spectacular growth later on. In this example, after year 10, the extra return earned on the accumulated investment earnings amounts to $267.10. By year 20, this amount increases over five-fold to $1,470 and after 50 years this amount reaches an astounding $24,957. And these are the earnings from setting aside $1,000 of savings only in the first year.

'A COOL TRILLION'

The *Research Reports* issue of May 21, 2007, featured an article on the costs of combating global warming — a topic raised by the release of the Intergovernmental Panel on Climate Change's Fourth Assessment Report in February of that year. The *Research Reports* article, titled, "A Cool Trillion," summarized: "Some estimates of the costs of reducing atmospheric carbon concentrations to levels which could avoid 'dangerous climate change' exceed $1 trillion per year. This might be money well spent, but if we wish to leave future generations with the highest living standards possible, such sacrifice may be imprudent."

An excerpt from the article:

The Money Costs of Doing Something

Meaningful climate mitigation is expected to cost 1.7 percent of world output according to the IPCC. With world GDP estimated at $65 trillion, this amounts to spending $1.1 trillion *each year* — larger than all but 15 of the world's economies — to potentially avert an increase in temperatures of 3.7 degrees. The Carbon Tax Center, a nonprofit think tank dedicated to promoting the importance of increasing carbon taxes, estimates that the direct per capita costs of mitigation would range from $2,400 per year for the poorest 20 percent of Americans to $8,700 per year for the wealthiest 20 percent (since they use more carbon). To compare, per capita federal income taxes in 2006 were $4,000.

Even if Americans could be convinced to make a sacrifice of this magnitude, success in preventing warming is far from guaranteed. There are major political hurdles — politicians must have the requisite knowledge and willpower to assess proper penalties on carbon emissions.

A bigger obstacle, however, is that to meaningfully reduce atmospheric carbon levels requires the cooperation of virtually every nation — particularly challenging given that 75 percent of carbon emissions in the next quarter-century are expected to come from poor developing countries. For example, China agreed to cut sulfur dioxide emissions by 10 percent in 2002, but today its emissions are 27 percent *higher*. For poor countries, the benefits of industrializing may be worth the uncertain long-term costs of global warming.

Cooperation from the rich countries is just as important. The Kyoto Protocol, the first global effort to curb emissions, was substantially less restrictive than current proposals, but still has fallen apart in Europe. Participating countries have issues so many "emissions permits" that carbon is "trading" at one Euro per ton, when its economic damage is supposedly closer to 50 Euro. Orders by the European Union to scale back the number of permits issued have been rejected by Germany. America has (in)famously chosen not to participate at all. Given these complications, and the mottled record of past global development initiatives, it is difficult to believe that 192 nations can successfully implement a multi-trillion dollar century-long policy.

Throwing a Wet Blanket on Growth

Even if it were politically and technically possible to spend $1.1 trillion to mitigate global warming each year, this does not mean it would be worth it. The relevant question is, what would society give up by dedicating resources to climate change policy?

We would be giving up a remarkable amount of economic growth. This large cost is one reason that activists must focus on extreme scenarios (such as the possibility that Manhattan Island will be overcome by the rising seas of a warmer planet) just to raise our collective consciousness to do something. To appreciate the magnitude of these proposed tradeoffs, consider if similar sacrifices had been made by our forebears 100 years ago. GDP currently stands at $13 trillion, roughly $44,000 per person. Had it grown by 1.7 percent less than it actually did from 1907 to 2006, GDP would be only 17 percent of today's output. At $2.3 trillion overall, per capita GDP would be $7,600 — well below the poverty line by today's standards, slightly above the $6,500 which prevailed in 1907, roughly equivalent to current living standards in countries like Botswana, Tunisia and Colombia.

Would you rather have $44,000 per person and live on a warm planet or $7,600 and live on a cooler planet? This is no idle question. Prosperity saves lives and substantially improves the human condition. Since 1900 U.S. life expectancy at birth has increased by 30 years, from 47 to 77; the real price of milk has fallen over 80 percent. In 1900, 15 percent of families had a flush toilet; 3 percent had electricity; 5 percent had a telephone; 1 percent had a car. Today these are well over 90 percent. Even the wealthiest "robber barons" could not instantly grab a cold drink — there were no refrigerators; they could not escape summer heat in air-conditioning; nor get penicillin to ward off infection, or even take an aspirin to relieve a headache. The economic value of health improvements alone since 1970 has been placed at $10 trillion in America, according to Kevin Murphy, a University of Chicago economist.

Would anyone have been willing to give up these advances in exchange for a reduction in global temperatures of 0.7 degrees (the actual increase in 20th century temperatures)? Would anyone make a similar exchange going forward, particularly when billions of the world's poorest stand to realize the biggest improvements to health and life expectancy from future economic growth?

CONCLUSION
TOWARD THE NEXT 75 YEARS

> "Although Colonel Harwood may never have been able to predict the changes to, and complexity of, today's financial product and services, one thing is clear — AIER's mission and products have never been more relevant and important than they are today."
>
> — *From a marketing study by Zone 5, 2006*

A market-research study conducted for the American Institute for Economic Research in 2006 by the Zone 5 firm, based in Albany, New York, began its executive summary with a quote from Alan Greenspan in 2003, when he was chairman of the Federal Reserve Board:

"Today's financial world is highly complex when compared with that of a generation ago. Forty years ago, a simple understanding of how to maintain a checking and savings account at local banks may have been enough. Now, consumers must be able to differentiate between a wide range of financial products and services, and providers of those products and services. Previous, less-indebted generations may not have needed a comprehensive understanding of such aspects of credit as the impact of compounding interest and the implications of

mismanaging credit accounts.

"Building bridges between community organizations, education institutions, and private businesses is essential to increasing familiarity with new technological and financial tools. And the success of such efforts will bear significantly on how well prepared our society is to meet the challenges of an increasingly knowledge-based economy.

" . . . let us remember that education is the primary means for creating new economic and financial opportunity for everyone. If we are able to boost our investment in people, ideas, and processes, just as we do in machines and technology, consumers and the economy can readily adapt to change, providing ever-rising standards of living for all Americans."

The executive summary of the market-

> **"For a while, we were somewhat insular and not necessarily recognized among the academic community and researchers. We want to make sure we're known among our peers for doing quality work."**
>
> — *Charles Murray, AIER president and CEO*

research study said that Greenspan's points "seem to be neatly aligned with the mission and vision of the American Institute for Economic Research, which was crafted 70 years earlier. Although Colonel Harwood may never have been able to predict the changes to, and complexity of, today's financial product and services, one thing is clear — AIER's mission and products have never been more relevant and important than they are today."

Those words would have sat well with the Institute's founder. In 1980, the year, Col. Harwood passed on, he wrote the following:

"The trustees have adopted a policy that requires budgeting for expenditures over a 10-year period both principal and interest on even the largest contribution. If AIER continues to survive it will be because its services to the public are valued in the decades ahead as clearly as they now are. As of 1980, the Reserved Life Income contributions for which AIER is trustee total more than $80 million and those held by Progress Foundation exceed $30 million. The total of $10 million is more than I had estimated to be necessary many years ago for the job to be done. It will be coming to AIER and to Progress Foundation at an average rate of nearly $2 million a year for decades. Thus the stage has at last been reached where we can view our long-range goal with reason to hope that consistently rapid progress toward it can be made.

"To summarize: The objective is to encourage teaching and application of useful procedures of inquiry to the problems of men in society to all the social sciences. Unless this goal is achieved in the next century or perhaps two, we see little reason to believe that the present civilization will survive rather than decline as have all the civilizations that have gone before. If the retrogression already apparent continues, how can the descent to another 'Dark Age' be avoided?" ❖

1) The patio on a side of the Castle is a popular congregation point for barbecues and other social events. 2) A rear view of Cotswold — popularly known as the Castle — AIER's home since 1946. 3) The Edward C. Harwood Library was remodeled in 2002, and its 20,000 square feet on two stories house administrative offices, a special economics library, classrooms, lecture hall and a 100-seat auditorium. 4) The views from the Castle are stunning, from the rolling Berkshire Hills to the Taconic Range. 5) A winding, mile-long road leads from Division Street up through forested land and to the driveway of the Castle. 6) Long Pond borders AIER's estate, and is a private water supply for neighboring villages.

CONCLUSION

1) The main hall of the Castle reflects the elegant tastes of Prentice Coonley, who built (though never finished) his dream house. 2) The first-floor TV room in the Castle offers respite to scholars and instructors. Movies with cultural or historical significance and documentaries frequently are shown in summer evenings in the room. 3) A circular staircase connects the first and second floors of the Castle, and provides exercise for the scholars rooming at the house. 4) The kitchen is kept busy year-round, feeding staff, visiting fellows and speakers, and conference attendees who room in the Castle or nearby cottages. 5) Originally intended as the master suite, and later occupied by E.C. Harwood's family, guest rooms on the second and third floor of the Castle offer dormitory accommodations for visiting scholars. 6) The research library contains materials spanning AIER's 75-year history and beyond — a resource for visiting scholars and fellows.

In the year 2000 alone, AIER's printing plant printed nearly 9 million impressions, and produced and mailed some 6 million circulars, nearly 300,000 Research Reports and some 190,000 bound books. AIER is one of the largest providers of private economic education in the United States.

The books, originally written as Economic Education Bulletins, are printed in a no-frills paperback format with black-and-white ink (no color) to keep costs down. List prices range from $3 to $12. The books can be ordered by calling the AIER Bookstore at (413) 528-1216, or by visiting the online bookstore at www.aier.org/bookstore.

The titles fall into four general categories: Personal Finance; Retirement Planning; Money and Banking; General Economics. A sampling:

Personal Finance

- Coin Buyer's Guide
- Homeowner or Tenant? How to Make a Wise Choice
- How to Avoid Financial Fraud
- How to Avoid Financial Tangles
- How to Give Wisely
- How to Invest Wisely

- How to Make Tax-Saving Gifts
- How to Read a Financial Statement
- How to Use Credit Wisely
- Life Insurance: From the Buyer's Point of View
- Sensible Budgeting With The Rubber Budget Account Book
- The A-Z Vocabulary for Investors
- What You Need To Know about Mutual Funds
- What Your Car Really Costs: How to Keep a Financially Safe Driving Record

Retirement Planning

- How to Build Wealth with Tax-Sheltered Investments
- How to Choose Retirement Housing
- How to Cover the Gaps in Medicare
- How to Plan for Your Retirement Years
- How to Produce Savings in the Administration of an Estate
- The Estate Plan Book
- What You Need To Know About Social Security
- Money and Banking
- Gold and Liberty
- Money: Its Origins, Development, Debasement, and Prospects
- Prospects For A Resumption Of The Gold Standard
- The Collapse of Deposit Insurance

General Economics

- On the Gap Between the Rich and the Poor
- Reconstruction of Economics
- The AIER Chart Book
- The United States Constitution: From Limited Government to Leviathan

The books provide practical financial information, in clear and concise English, for the individual and small investor. Following are excerpts from two of the books:

From *What Your Car Really Costs: How to Keep a Financially Safe Driving Record*:

Should You Buy New or Used?

The surge in new car sales, spurred by attractive sales incentives, has created a bumper crop of late-model used cars. Millions of cars are traded in every year, many of them with relatively low mileage. In addition, millions of vehicles are returned to dealer lots each year when their leases expire. Because of stipulations in the contract, leased cars are usually well kept and in much better condition than the fleet cars that used-car buyers had to settle for in the past.

Not only do used-car buyers have a wider range of cars to choose from, but the cars are not physically depreciating as fast as they did years ago. Presumably, this is partly due to the better build of cars generally, the higher quality of previously leased cars on the market, and the fact that leases limit the number of miles someone can drive a car without adding cost to the lease.

The glut of used cars and this improvement in quality means that it is possible to get a good deal on a two- or three-year-old used car. For example, our tables show that the 2002 Buick Regal, one of *Consumer Reports'* recommended use cars, currently sells for just 46 percent of its original M.S.R.P. The 2001 Buick Regal, which is also recommended, is selling for 38 percent of its original sticker price. . . .

The trend toward longer warranties also has made used cars more attractive. The standard bumper-to-bumper warranty used to run for three years or 36,000 miles. But some automakers now offer them for four years and 50,000 miles, or even longer. Powertrain warranties, which cover the car's engine and transmission, may run as long as ten years or

100,000 miles. In addition, many warranties can be transferred from one owner to the next (check before you buy a used car). Some used cars that have been "certified" by car makers carry additional warranties (for example, Toyota's certified vehicles carry a seven-year, 100,000 limited factory warranty).

In today's market, used car buyers probably will find it relatively easy to find a "recommended" late-model car selling at a good discount from its original price. Even if you can afford a new car, the current "low" resale prices of cars would seem to favor used car purchases over new car purchases. Of course, there still are bargains to be had on new cars. Whether buying new or used, we recommend that car shoppers consult the April auto issue of *Consumer Reports*, which lists new and used cars that are "good bets."

* * *

From *How to Plan for Your Retirement Years*:

Retirement Strategies
in Financial Perspective

There is a simple rule to remember about saving for retirement. Save as much as you can as soon as you are financially able to do so, because the "magic of compounding" is much more powerful over longer periods of time. Consider that if you save $1,000 a year in an account earning 8 percent, you will have about $79,000 after 25 years (before taxes). After 10 years, using the same assumptions, the balance would be only about $16,000. . . .

Another way to make this same point appears in Table 1, which shows how large a sum even modest monthly savings can generate, if you start early.

Table 1: How Much You Need to Invest to Reach $100,000 at Retirement (Savings in a tax-deferred account earning an 8 percent rate of return)		
Contributions made from age …	Monthly contribution	Total Contribution
25 to 65	$29	$13,920
30 to 65	$44	$18,480
35 to 65	$67	$24,120
40 to 65	$105	$31,500
45 to 65	$170	$40,800
50 to 65	$289	$52,020
55 to 65	$547	$65,640

CHAPTER A

Given our culture of consumption, setting aside even modest amounts is often easier said than done. In addition to paying for the necessities of life, people spend money on everything from flat-screen television sets to luxury cars to resort vacations for the family. Saving for retirement is often an afterthought.

In any case, financial priorities will no doubt shift during the course of your income-earning years. At some points, immediate needs such as buying a house or funding a child's education may seem more important than setting aside money for a retirement that may be years, or even decades, away.

Once you meet the primary responsibilities at the various stages of your "financial life," however, you should address your expected retirement needs and decide how to provide for them. One of the best ways to do this is to automatically set aside either a percentage of earnings or a specific dollar amount each month, through payroll deduction at your place of work or through the automatic investment plans offered by many brokers and mutual fund firms. A systematic saving and investment program changes retirement saving from an afterthought to a regular, fixed expense. ❖

APPENDIX B
CHARITABLE GIVING SUSTAINS AIER

The American Institute for Economic Research holds nonprofit 501(c)3 status, and contributions to the Institute are deductible for its charitable tax purposes. These donations ensure the Institute's survival and continued diligent work to carry out its vital mission of providing the public with the most objective research on the economy, and providing individuals with the information and advice they need to guard and grow their financial assets.

In line with its tradition begun 75 years ago at its founding, AIER operates with a lean professional staff dedicated to keeping costs to customers down. The Institute's audience continues to build; in 2007, AIER mailed nearly 5 million marketing circulars, 200,000 Economic Education Bulletin *booklets, and 250,000* Research Reports. *The Institute ranks among the largest providers of private economic education in the nation. AIER's summer fellowship program, nurturing a new generation of scientifically minded economists, in 2007 featured an unprecedented breadth and depth of expertise among teachers and speakers. And AIER conducted an intensive market research study to determine new*

bases of customers who will benefit from the Institute's work in the years ahead.

Even with increased sales of products, charitable contributions cover more than two-thirds of the Institute's annual operating budget. The Institute's strict independence, protected by its bylaws, prohibits accepting gifts from private foundations, commercial interests or the government. Therefore, continued support from individual friends — those who understand and appreciate the importance of the independent economic perspective AIER offers — is critical to the Institute's survival. This invaluable support allows AIER to keep its products affordable to the average citizen even as the Institute expands its programs and resists constant inflationary pressure.

The simplest method for making deferred gifts to AIER is for a donor to include the Institute in his or her will, through a bequest, or by making the Institute a beneficiary in a life-insurance policy.

A special program of charitable giving has greatly assisted AIER's long-term success. Donors transfer property to the Institute as a trustee and remainderman, but reserve a life income interest for themselves and designated *beneficiaries. By 2007, the market value of assets held in these trusts exceeded $150 million. As the remainderman portion becomes available to the Institute, its continuing scientific and educational efforts can expand accordingly. This program also can benefit a donor in a variety of ways. The donor may qualify for federal or state income-tax deductions. The donor can receive, or have beneficiaries receive, annual income for life or a designated term. The donor may save capital-gain taxes on a gift of appreciated assets. And the gift will benefit AIER's expert asset management.*

The Institute's prudent fund management has provided a steady stream of income to beneficiaries for many years while achieving many tax-saving objectives. The Institute offers three institutional planned giving programs:

Reserved Life Income Funds. RLI is a pooled income fund. When a donor makes an irrevocable gift of cash or securities gift to the RLI, it is invested with the gifts of all other fund donors. Each quarter, the donor's proportional share of the fund's income is distributed to the beneficiaries the donor has named. The income distribution varies with the fund's performance. When the last beneficiary dies, the principal attributable to the gift is removed from the RLI fund and given to AIER, to be used for its charitable purposes. Donors may add funds to their RLI at any time.

Charitable Remainder Unitrusts. A CRU is an income fund where donations are not pooled with other donations. Donors stipulate a fixed percentage (not less than 5 percent) of the value of the fund to be distributed annually to the income beneficiaries. Income may continue for the lifetimes of the beneficiaries named, a fixed term of not more than 20 years, or a combination of the two. Payments are made out of trust income, or trust principal if income is not adequate. When the CRU term ends, the principal passes to AIER for its charitable programs. Donors may add funds to their CRU at any time.

Charitable Gift Annuity. A CGA is a contract (not a trust), under which AIER, in return for a transfer of cash, marketable securities or other assets, agrees to pay a fixed amount of money to one or two individuals, for their lifetime, not a term of years. Annuity payments are fixed and unchanged for the term of the contract. The contributed property, given irrevocably, becomes a part of the charity's assets, and the payments are a general obligation of the charity. That means the annuity is backed by the charity's entire assets, not just by the property contributed. The donor must be first annuitant, but can also name a second annuitant. CGAs may offer immediate or deferred payouts.

More information on AIER's planned giving programs is available on the website — *www.aier.org/support*. Information also is available by emailing *PlannedGiving@aier.org*; or by writing to Shaun Buckler, CFO, P.O. Box 1000, Great Barrington, MA 01230. ❖

THE FOULKE FAMILY: LEAVING A LASTING LEGACY AT AIER

The Foulke family has made a lasting legacy of contributions to the American Institute for Economic Research. Roy Anderson Foulke, Sr., was a personal friend of Institute founder Col. E.C. Harwood, and served as a board trustee from 1963 to 1972, chairman of the board from 1966 to 1972, and thereafter as a lifetime member, and honorary chairman, of AIER Corp.

Foulke brought vast business experience to the Institute. A Phi Beta Kappa graduate of Bowdoin College, in Brunswick, Maine, and a World War I veteran, he went on to become vice president of Dun & Bradstreet and to author five volumes and numerous articles dealing with financial and business analysis. He developed a method of norms and ratios — which became widely used — for comparing strengths and weaknesses of companies in the same line of business.

Roy Anderson Foulke, Sr., a longtime friend of Col. Harwood, chaired AIER's corporate board for seven years and helped amend the corporate declaration to preserve the Institute's nonprofit status in a dispute with the IRS. Foulke was a personal friend of Col. Harwood's and was made honorary chairman of AIER's corporation.

Foulke's expertise in finance and his utter devotion to AIER's welfare proved themselves in resolving a crisis the Institute encountered in 1965, after the Internal Revenue Service revoked AIER's tax-exempt status. It was a serious blow; the Institute had mailed its circulars and publications at preferred nonprofit rates, and had operated pooled-income funds. Foulke and other colleagues who were voting members found themselves at odds with some staff and faculty who wanted to change AIER's nonprofit mission into that of a moneymaking organization selling financial advice. But Foulke's group prevailed, and he and others on the corporate board signed the necessary articles of amendment to the Institute's corporate declaration. This created a separate for-profit investment-advisory service, and also brought AIER in line with the Internal Revenue Code's Section 501(c)3 for charitable nonprofit organizations. Fittingly, one of AIER's first reserved life income funds was named the Roy A. Foulke Fund.

The next generation of Foulkes performed its own invaluable service to the Institute. Roy

APPENDIX B

139

The Foulke Family: From left, Maureen Foulke; late husband, Roy, .Jr.; son, John; daughter, Sarah. The Foulkes have been stalwart supporters of AIER for decades. Roy, Jr., chaired the board of the American Investment Services for eight years. Maureen, John and Sarah continue as AIER voting members. The Foulke Foundation awards an annual scholarship to promising student fellows at the Institute.

Anderson Foulke, Jr. (1927-1999) was a longtime voting member. A graduate of Bowdoin College with a master's of business administration from Stanford, Foulke forged a successful career in finance and industry. In 1978 he was the founding director of American Investment Services, Inc., and chaired the AIS board for eight years. In 1987 he was elected to AIER's board of trustees and chaired that body from 1995 until his death.

Even in the Institute's darkest days — when the U.S. Securities and Exchange Commission was suing AIER and its affiliates, Col. Harwood and other officers over alleged infractions of federal laws — the Foulke family stood steadfastly in the ranks of AIER supporters. As Maureen Foulke, wife of the late Roy, Jr., said, "Roy and his father were involved with economics and finance, and felt that AIER represented their feelings about how one should invest as free marketers."

AIER's research and advice provide incalculable value to those who heed it, Maureen Foulke noted. She cited the example of a friend of her husband's. The friend was an international banker whose investing results were less than favorable. "Roy told him about AIER's research and counsel, and how to go about investing. It's not done with big swings, it's one foot in front of the other. And it benefited the man enormously. He ended up dying of cancer, but before his death he told Roy that he'd never have had an estate left by the time the doctors got through with him if Roy hadn't shown him what to do."

Maureen Foulke and her son, John, and daughter, Sarah, continue as AIER voting members. The Foulke Foundation, in memory of Roy A. Foulke, Jr., annually awards a $10,000 scholarship to an AIER student fellow or fellows demonstrating the highest potential for development in practicing economic science dedicated to finding solutions to human problems, in AIER's tradition.

Maureen Foulke sees AIER's mission as remaining as vital as ever and hopes its officers "stick to their guns and continue doing what they're doing, the way that Col. Harwood and Roy's father and Roy directed it. There's always a danger, when you have an institute in a small town, that it can get smaller instead of growing. I'm hoping it will grow to be a bigger institute with wider representation among people — not just those using the Institute to invest, but those who advise the Institute. I'm hoping it will grow and reach a greater audience, and greater participation among experts who are actually in the market, managing investing. I hope its research will have more support from the people doing the advising, and using all its economic and investing principles."

APPENDIX C

THE FREE-FLOWING PEN OF E.C. HARWOOD: THREE ESSAYS

E.C. Harwood's restless mind continuously flowed with creative thought throughout his life, and his penchant for committing his convictions and musings to ink produced hundreds of articles and essays, and nine full-length books.

A fair representation of his wide-ranging writings would fill many pages, so we will suffice to reprint three shorter pieces in this appendix. The first, "The Full Significance of Freedom," was published in *The American Journal of Economics and Sociology* in 1945. The version appearing below was edited and condensed by Fred Harwood. The remaining two essays — "Down with the Radio, the Opiate of the People" (written in 1930), and "The Menace of the American Suburb" (written sometime in the mid-1930s) — may never have seen the light of publication. That is, copies of typewritten drafts are preserved in the AIER library, but they are not accompanied by notes indicating whether they landed in a journal or other publication.

The trio of essays demonstrate not only the fertility of E.C. Harwood's ponderings, but his strident and whimsical sides, as well. They also illustrate his keen analysis of society that remains relevant today. Points raised in "The Full Significance of Freedom" bring into question the entitlement mentality of contemporary American Society. One can easily substitute "television" or "Internet" for the "radio" in the essay, "Down with the Radio, the Opiate of the People." And the dream world of the affluent suburb, described in, "The Menace of the American Suburb," continues to nurture a class of people, including young people, possessed of what Harwood termed "a distorted conception of life's realities."

* * *

"THE FULL SIGNIFICANCE OF FREEDOM"

(Edited and condensed by Fred Harwood)

Ever since John Stuart Mill wrote his famous essay "On Liberty," few reasoning persons can doubt that freedom of thought, belief, and expression is an essential ingredient of individual freedom. The Civil War established in the United States that the ownership of one human being by another could not be tolerated in a free society. This finding has been extended by most of the rest of the world as its peoples, coming to understand what freedom means, have grasped at it. In our country, our

Constitution recognizes, have seen that freedom for the individual includes inalienable rights or defenses against even the most powerful state or federal government — defenses that long-established customs have made an integral part of our legal procedure.

Individual freedom is the acknowledged primary aim of our form of government. This form was based on the assumption that individual freedom makes for responsible actions because authority to act implies responsibility for the consequences of the act. Moreover, such responsibility leads to the cultivation of judgment, ability, and character. Finally, the best society, the one most fitted to endure in the long run, is one consisting of the most highly developed individuals rather than one composed of the slaves of an all-powerful state.

Sometimes forgotten is that enslavement of the individual must inevitably make him irresponsible and thereby retard growth of judgment, ability, and character. The childlike gayety of the slaves we had in our country long ago was frequently construed as the acme of happiness (although no free men seemed eager to enjoy that happiness by sharing their bondage). But the plain truth is that humans not permitted to assume the responsibilities of adults must remain children. And our Constitution implicitly assumes that the best society will result when citizens are permitted and encouraged to become responsible adults.

When this theory of society was first elaborated and put into practice, it was scoffed at as a theory that had not been tested by experience. More than a century and a half has elapsed since then, however, and the strongest conceivable proof that the theory is sound confronts us. In this relatively short period of history, the nation has grown, and civilization within the United States has flourished. We have leaped ahead of the great industrial nations of Europe, one after another, in our ability to create what mankind wants; art and science have benefited on a scale beyond the imagination of the peoples of the Old World; and our progress has surpassed the comprehension of the vast populations of India and Asia. That this great advance of civilization was attributable neither to greater natural resources nor to a basically more intelligent people is evident; Europe, South America, Africa and China each has natural resources that exceed those of the United States. Our people are descendants of European stocks, for the most part. There remains only the great difference in application of the principle of freedom to account for the flowering of civilization in the United States.

I

Nevertheless, few believe that our society in the United States is perfect. It is unnecessary to describe its defects in detail, so apparent are they. Consequently, one is forced to conclude either that our fundamental theory of the good society is unsound or that we have failed in part to apply that basic theory.

Some have accepted the first alternative and would turn back the clock of history and establish a society in our country in which the individual would be less free and more a chattel of the state (as has occurred in some nations of Europe during our time). Rarely do we find such thoughts given clear expression, but they are to be judged rather by actions than words; and the actions of many clearly show that they either never have understood or no longer believe in the principle of freedom for the individual. Before we accede to the desires of these backward-looking individuals, we should consider the alternative possibility that we have failed in part to apply the theory of freedom and therefore may find our goal further along the road we have traveled rather than somewhere back upon it.

At first glance, our concept of freedom seems to be complete. We choose those who govern our cities, states, and the nation; we have reasonably well-observed Constitutional defenses against usurpation of individual rights by the government; and we have freedom of religion, thought, and expression. There is some talk of freedom from fear, but every adult mind knows that there will never be freedom from fear in general, although there already is freedom from some fears in particular. Some also talk of freedom from want, but most people realize that those who are free to dispose of their goods as they please can never be guaranteed freedom from want; valuable slaves are the only human beings who have ever had this freedom. (Possibly even these wanted more than they received.) What then, if any, is the additional feature or features of the principle of freedom that may have been overlooked?

Sometimes, when an idea is difficult to grasp in all its aspects, think of its opposite. In this way we may find a clue to the elusive application.

The opposite of freedom is slavery. Aside from the loss of freedoms already discussed, what are other important features of slavery? They become obvious when we ask why humans have been enslaved.

The one most compelling reason for some to enslave others apparently has always been so that a master could require the slaves to work for the master without giving them in return more than part of the fruits of their labor. To put the matter bluntly, chattel slavery was, and still is in parts of the world, legalized robbery, a means by which some men are forced to live a part of their lives for the benefit of masters. From this fact, we may draw the conclusion that, when some are privileged to take from others part of the fruits of their labor without recompense in kind or in corresponding value, to precisely that extent those whose wealth is thus appropriated are slaves.

Inasmuch as slavery in any degree is the negation of freedom, it is apparent that the theory of freedom also implies that everyone should receive the fruits of one's labor, either in kind or in corresponding value. Possibly some will assume that the freedom to make employment contracts, which citizens of the United States have to a marked degree, automatically prevents any interference with freedom to retain the fruits of one's labor. If one thinks one's efforts are worth more than one gets for them, one is at liberty to resign one's employment and seek other work for which one may be adequately compensated. Of course, freedom to seek does not guarantee finding, but most citizens probably believe that, as a practical matter, one can find a full reward for one's services if one will but seek diligently enough, except perhaps in occasional periods of business depression.

The question therefore becomes, is this general assumption true or is a substantial part of our society actually deprived of a portion of the fruits of their labor and to that extent enslaved?

Again we can more readily gain enlightenment by considering the reverse of the picture.

Nothing more than ability to add and subtract is needed to prove that, when some are robbed of the fruits of their labor, the appropriators get something for nothing; at least they get something without giving in exchange its full equivalent value. It follows, then, that if some in a society are able to get something for nothing, others must be getting nothing for something. We must therefore ask, are there people in the United States who are able to get something for nothing?

The answer to this seems obvious; thousands, perhaps millions, of persons in the United States get something for nothing. The more conspicuously fortunate of this class constitute part of the idle rich, which class of persons show successive gradations of fortune.

II

Lest the foregoing be misunderstood, we must distinguish carefully between three classes of the wealthy. Unfortunately, the usual reaction of the underdog is to resent all wealth, earned or unearned. The three groups we considered are:

1. Those who have earned their wealth and large incomes by extraordinary ability. Such a man as Henry Ford, perhaps, would be in this group.

2. Those who have inherited wealth that represents a reward for work done by their ancestors. The younger Edison is perhaps an example of this class.

3. Those who have acquired, by inheritance or otherwise, monopoly privileges of one sort or another which enable them to demand an income without giving anything in return. The present generation of the Astor family, to some extent, is an example of this class.

The first group gives value received for its incomes, and therefore cause no one to be deprived of the fruits of their labor. It is not so easy for many people to understand that those in the second group likewise give value received. That they do so is clear if they simply spend the funds (dissipate the capital) accumulated by their ancestors. But what if they live on the interest or dividends from securities representing buildings or manufacturing plants produced by their ancestors?

The early religious view was that all interest was usury and all usury was sin, a robbing of the needy by the rich. This is still the Socialist point of view. However, now well established is that capital in the form of buildings, machines, factories, et cetera, is itself a partner in the productive process and earns its share of the product. If this is so, the individuals in the second group do not have the power to appropriate the fruits of the labor of others without an equivalent return.

Now capital (defined as that part of tangible wealth or goods used for the production of more goods) is wealth (goods) in the process of manufacture and exchange; that is, it is wealth (goods) not yet placed, in its entirety, in the hands of the ultimate consumer. To illustrate:

1. Cattle on the range are capital goods part way along in the overall process of production and exchange.

2. A manufacturing plant is a form of capital, which is in some stage of a gradual conversion to goods for the ultimate consumer. A lathe wears out as it is used to make wooden spindles for chair rungs. This product, therefore, has embodied in it both the human effort immediately involved and the human effort originally devoted to making the lathe. Making the lathe, in effect, stores up human effort in a certain form that can be converted into other products farther along toward the ultimate consumer. Such capital is thus in the process of production and exchange.

3. A merchant's inventory or stock of goods for sale is obviously in the process of production and exchange en route to the ultimate consumer.

The process of exchange makes possible more efficient production of goods because it enables human effort to specialize in types of work yielding the maximum product in each locality. The lumbermen of the Pacific Northwest can produce lumber with relatively little human effort, compared with the effort involved in growing and cutting timber in Kansas. The farmers of Kansas can grow wheat with less human effort per bushel than wheat could be grown in the lumber areas of the Pacific Northwest, where even extensive clearing to prepare the fields would not better the climate for wheat growing. Provided that more wheat is grown than consumed in Kansas and more lumber is cut than is used in the Pacific Northwest, a mutually advantageous exchange can be made for the obvious reason that the farmers and the lumbermen thus share a much larger total production of wealth (goods) than they would have if each farmer spent some of his time growing trees and sawing them and each lumberman took time from lumbering to clear fields and cultivate wheat.

Note that capital is required for this purpose. Some wheat and some lumber must be saved (not consumed immediately) and placed in the channels of exchange. En route, some of the lumber may become furniture as a result of adding capital and human effort to it; and the wheat may become flour, which then includes the original wheat plus the human effort of the miller plus that part of the milling machinery (a portion of its useful life) used in making the flour.

Capital goods thus contribute toward the final product for the consumer. Capital contributes the human effort stored up in the factory or other capital goods. In addition capital contributes the increase in the total product that results from specialization with consequent greater product per unit of human effort.

It follows that individuals who provide capital goods can be given the equivalent value of those goods in the form of a share of the final product plus an additional portion of the final product or its money value representing the added production made possible by the use of this capital. In other words, the one who owns a machine can take enough of the money value of the product to compensate oneself for wearing out the machine plus some more without taking any of that part of the product directly attributable to the later contribution of human effort made by the operator of the machine. And whether the owner of the machine built it himself or inherited it from some ancestor does not matter.

The additional amount paid to the owner of the factory, over and above that needed to buy a new factory when the existing one is worn out, is usually called interest, or sometimes, dividends. (However, the interest on some bonds, say a government bond, is not of this character for obvious reasons; and dividends paid from monopoly gains are also not of this character.)

So, although those who inherit capital get something for nothing, they get it only at the expense of the ancestor whose effort created the capital; and the interest or dividends received subsequently come not from the share of the product attributable to the efforts of the factory operatives, but from the additional product made possible by the existence of capital goods (i.e., wealth in the process of production and exchange). Interest and dividends of this character therefore do not deprive those currently applying their human effort in the productive processes of their full share of the ultimate product.

III

Equally clear, however, is that the income derived from a monopoly privilege must ordinarily be at the expense of those devoting their human effort to the production of goods. Consequently, all who get something for nothing as a result of owing monopoly privileges of one sort or another are in effect and to a degree enslaving their fellows who work for a living. To the extent that some are forced to give up part of the value of their effort applied in production, they are enslaved. Do such conditions actually exist? An example will prove that they do.

More than 150 years ago, George III, then King of England, by a stroke of the pen and for no real value received gave certain favorites some monopoly privileges in the New World. Today, the descendants of those favored individuals have an absolute monopoly privilege to demand a substantial fee for the use of hundreds of thousands of acres of the finest farmland in the Middle West. If they choose, they may prohibit the cultivation of the land, even though the produce of it may be needed for food to keep people from starving. Ordinarily, however, the monopoly privilege is used to obtain a share of the product, and the share thus obtainable usually is nearly all that portion of the crop which is over and above the crops that can be produced at the margin of cultivation where crop yields are low in proportion to the human effort expended. Any would-be farmer who will not pay this large share of the produce for the privilege of using the better land has no alternative but to labor for still less on the nearest free land available.

In some instances, the monopoly privileges apply to areas within growing cities. What was once open prairie becomes a center of productive activity; railroads are provided by capitalists, thereby making it a center for advantageous exchanges; roads built by county, state, and federal governments facilitate local shipments and exchanges; people congregate there, thus providing a pool of potential workers, a good labor market; large numbers of consumers live there; they build churches, schools, theaters, and other attractions that bring still more people because life is pleasanter there; and capitalists find it advantageous to manufacture in this locality where labor and consumers have congregated. What does this do for the holder of a monopoly privilege?

Here is a specific instance. A single plot of land, perhaps an acre, is in an American city, but the descendant of a king's favorite holds the monopoly privilege, the right to say, "If you wish to use this space on the surface of the Earth, pay me (in this instance) $235,000 annually." And a large corporation is paying this fee, although the holder of the monopoly privilege has written in the contract that the company, at the end of 30 years, must tear down any building erected and give up the use of this space if the holder of the monopoly privilege so desires!

This is but one of millions of such instances. What the grand total of the takings based on such privileges would be, no one knows, but it is a substantial share of current production.

Here then is the proof that hundreds of thousands of those who apply their efforts of brain or hand in production are deprived of a portion of what they produce. In effect, part of their time is devoted to making goods for holders of monopoly privileges who give no return for value received. For the indicated portion of their lives, those applying effort in production are, in effect, enslaved; and to precisely that extent are they deprived of their freedom.

In at least one important respect, we have failed to continue on the road toward perfect freedom. We have stopped short of the goal, so much short that by far the most of the people of the United States spend a substantial portion of their lives in virtual slavery, bound by ties they do not understand, bonds strengthened by legal traditions and the growing economic power of the "masters" or owners of the widespread monopoly privilege. And the poorer classes of the population, little understanding the nature of their bondage but suffering its evil effects, follow any demagogue who offers them a hope of change in belief that any change, even a move backward toward the Dark Ages, will be a change for the better. Thus, men come to power who neither understand nor care for the principle of freedom that is the intended goal of our Constitution, and to satisfy the masses who elected them pass laws that reverse the movement toward freedom and take us back along the road on which mankind has struggled to move forward for hundreds of years.

Relatively easy to understand is that slavery, in effect and to a degree, still exists in the United States. It stunts growth, especially the intellectual development and sense of responsibility of a major portion of the population. It therefore may be the principal danger to our form of society and to our civilization. But the question is, What is the remedy; how can monopoly privileges of the character pointed out be ended without a complete disruption of the social system? Is this the all-important question to which we must find an answer or perish as have other civilizations before ours?

* * *

"DOWN WITH THE RADIO, THE OPIATE OF THE PEOPLE"

Events move so swiftly in Russia that it is somewhat difficult to recall the many wrangles we have had with that country. Everything those unfortunate individuals do seems to rub us the wrong way, whether it's growing whiskers or divorcing wives. (Is it possible that there is an element of jealousy in our righteous indignation?) At any event, in the not far distant past, many Americans were worried about Russia's attitude toward religion. Of course, the more recent shock to our pocketbook nerve via the wheat market has pushed the religious question far into the background. Now it is certainly not desired to resurrect that particular bogeyman, but Russia's methods at that time, its fanatical zeal in rooting out the people's opiate, demonstrates how simple a diversion is required to occupy the vast energies of professional reformers, et al. Then too, the very phrase, "opiate of the people," is extremely suggestive.

While we haven't as much to crusade against as Russia has, it may be possible to uncover an objective for our descendants of the Boston Tea Party, prohibitionists, and cast-off chamber of commerce secretaries. Having approached this closely to the subject, it now seems advisable to back off and come on another tack.

Consider the days of, well, of quite a long time ago; the date really doesn't matter. Life for the average man, and especially for the farmer was apt to get monotonous. After the crops were in, say by Thanksgiving, until spring plowing began, there was time to burn, so to speak. Apparently those sturdy ancestors used quite a bit of it for sleeping, eating, and testing the contents of that cider barrel down cellar. But those winter months were long and tedious. Christmas came as a great relief. Spelling bees helped to while away some of the hours (and if that doesn't prove that time was a little too much for them, what would?). In spite of everything, however, some of the long winter evenings would come along and catch Uncle Ned and Aunt Martha with not a single thing to do. At first, they bore up under the strain pretty well. Along into January one could always drop off for another 40 winks, and presto, it would be bedtime before you knew it.

February, though, was a different proposition. With spring just around the corner, people would get restless from too much rest. Unless something unusual happened, a body was almost sure to do a little Thinking before spring finally arrived. Everybody had been "settin' " so long that they would get desperate and start to "set and Think." Probably the Thinking those sturdy pioneers indulged in accounts for this country's progress to date. At least some of the politicians were statesmen. They had to be because almost every one of their constituents was Thinking, at least once in four years.

Well, conditions certainly have changed, and not for the better. The Census shows that some 13 million homes are equipped with radios. At an average of five persons to the family, that means there are about 65 million people in this country who don't know what Thinking is, not from recent experience anyway.

Even in our institutions of higher learning, the radio has crept in. It is customary now when a new dormitory is being built to install special connections in every room for radio reception. When the day's memorizing is done a student no longer needs to Think, or else run wild with the boys. He can just tune in on the radio, like the folks back home, and thus keep his grasshopper mind on the jump until Morpheus ends the agony of consciousness.

The dangers to the long-run welfare of the country are obvious. It is not to be wondered at that the demagogues get more demagogical; that prohibition gets more muddled with every added statistic; and that bootstrap lifting has become as popular as Bryan would have made it, even in a day when the bootstrap is no more.

The obvious solution of this grave problem which threatens our civilization is to cast out radio; to tear out of the sacred American home this time-consuming monster; to prohibit any public displays of these seductive eight tube super-something-dynes.

Down with the radio — the opiate of the people.

* * *

"THE MENACE OF THE AMERICAN SUBURB"

The American suburb is a real menace. Like many other institutions that have carelessly been permitted to develop in American social life, it fattens upon the evils which it creates. Unless its insidious growth is checked, and steps are taken to reverse the tendencies already in evidence, the American suburb will be responsible, to a substantial degree, for the decline of American civilization.

Twenty-five or 30 years ago, the outward trek of the suburban pioneers from large cities was but an insignificant forerunner of the developments to come. The individuals concerned were, for the most part, only a few of the moderately well-to-do whose nostalgia for country life and ways was assuaged by this seemingly harmless shift from city to suburb. In those days, the suburb had a distinctly rural atmosphere, and it was accepted as a matter of course that all suburbanites were innocuous, rubber-shod bipeds, perennially lost in the seed catalogues, and by their sophisticated city brethren suspected of having hayseed in their hair. It was generally felt that their removal from the city was good riddance, because, like fish out of water, they could not have contributed anything useful to the character of city life.

The striking change in the character of suburbs and suburbanites that has since occurred was made possible by the development of the automobile, and was greatly accelerated by the inflationary war and post-war decades.

APPENDIX C

151

During the latter period especially, the boom decade of the 1920s, the American suburb began to develop along lines and with results that can only be described as menacing. It was during those years that a major portion of the moderately successful white-collar class, including the nation's leaders in business and industry, large and small, joined the pilgrimage to suburban areas. The suburb lost its rural aspects and became a "citified" residential area, which was, however, a separate and distinct body from the metropolis that gave it birth.

There is no doubt that the progressive inflation that culminated in the 1929 boom and subsequent collapse was to a substantial degree responsible for the growth of the American suburb. The tendencies were in evidence well before that period, and the automobile would have done much to strengthen them. However, it seems probable that inflation can be blamed for the rapid acceleration of the process that, because of the speed of the changes involved, made compensating adjustments impossible. The stock market boom furnished the wherewithal, and the real estate boom provided the homes for those businessmen and executives who led the flight to the suburbs.

It has been argued that the American suburb is the most American feature of American life. Its defenders urge that in these areas we find a survival of the New England town meeting form of government, or its modern parallel, the representative town meeting. Most suburban towns and cities are well governed and have excellent schools. The percentage of foreign population is usually much less than in the nearby cities. Churches there are in abundance, and to those who do not probe beneath the surface, the American suburb seems the very core of American culture, and perhaps the best institution for preserving it in the future.

That such views are erroneous, and that they wholly overlook the threatening aspects of the flight to our suburbs, can easily be shown. It is true that the suburbs themselves offer much that is desirable in American life. But the important questions are: What kind of citizens are being produced in the suburban environment?; and, What is happening in the city that the suburbanites have abandoned?

The effect of suburban life on the youth in such localities can easily be imagined by those who have not actually seen it. Children are brought up in what virtually amounts to a classless community. They see little of the struggle for existence, and inevitably develop a distorted conception of life's realities. Through a complete lack of contact with nine-tenths of their fellow citizens, they fail to learn the stern lessons in economics that even the urchins who deliver your morning paper know.

It seems probable that this situation accounts for the ready acceptance of such ideas as the "surplus economy" and the over-savings theory of the business cycle. The youths nurtured in our unrealistic suburban environment, given a veneer called a college education, are ripe prospects for the parlor pinks and purveyors of the bootstrap-lifting brand of economics. Our unfortunate suburbanite striplings have as unrealistic an understanding of production and distribution problems as those of us who were brought up in the Mid-Victorian era had toward romance and babies: in other words, they drift on the vast, uncharted sea of ignorance in an impenetrable fog of idealism.

The effort made to fit the male youths for their places in the economic scheme is a logical outgrowth of the softening influences with which they are surrounded. At private day schools or modernized public schools, they are encouraged to develop their own personalities, while their teachers escape the boredom of the drill and discipline essential to the acquirement of genuine habits of study and a firm foundation for future work. Even those students who subsequently take the so-called business courses in graduate institutions, presumably intended to fit them for executive places in the economic scheme, become masters and doctors of business administration without benefit of more than elementary high school mathematics. Obviously, they must lack an adequate understanding of economic principles and processes; they cannot even comprehend the real significance of many simple charts of business statistics.

The young women who mature in the typical American suburb are even more seriously handicapped by its influence. It is no longer fashionable to sew garments for the naked heathen, but a multitude of equally silly causes sponsored by the daughters of suburbanites have been substituted.

At the schools provided for their higher education, many so-called "practical" courses are offered. Unfortunately, the noble art of thinking is all too frequently neglected. Hardly any of the young women given the right to vote could pass with credit even an examination based on Lewis Carroll's "Logical Nonsense."

Serious as this corruption of the young may be, it is in answering the second question that we find the most disturbing consequences of suburban development. That question was: "What is happening in the city that the suburbanites abandoned?"

A brief survey of any of several large cities in the country reveals what follows when the city's natural leaders abdicated by becoming mere suburbanites. The same thing happens that has always occurred when those in a natural position of leadership have refused to exercise that function. Other leaders interested primarily in self-aggrandizement jump to the front, and by the all too familiar methods of the demagogue, play upon the emotions of the multitude in order to win the emoluments of public office. Once having secured a place, the next step is to build a political machine, and from that time forward only a dispute between the gangsters and racketeers in control can effect any marked change in that city's slow progress toward bankruptcy. Even those changes seem to be singularly unimportant in the long run.

Until recently, the suburbanites have prided themselves on their wisdom and good fortune. Not for them were the penalties of high taxes and dirty politics. By afternoon-tea campaigns and other amateurish political efforts, they convinced themselves that in keeping the holy ground of their little village free from the mud of city politics, they were performing a Herculean task that entitled them to the reward of the righteous.

How puerile these efforts have been, and how insignificant is the protection that the suburbanites have gained, is now becoming apparent. Politicians with a broader vision have discovered that the masses in the cities, under the tutelage of their local gods of politics, can be induced to aid the one who promises most, especially if there is some measure of practical performance in the way of jobs and allotments. In other words, to paraphrase Mr. Farley, the cities have the votes.

It was not so many years ago that political affiliations were determined by one's birthplace. It would, of course, be silly to argue that birth rather than principles should be the determining factor in a choice of political parties. However, the arbitrary difference in environment created by the suburb versus city dividing line is an even less satisfactory determinant of political affiliations.

In the days when the manual laborers, the clerks, minor executives, and the boss himself all lived in the same city, there was a definite community of social interests and an exchange of ideas and beliefs that included the realm of politics, to some extent. No one knows better than their subordinates how valuable the judgments of business executives are. The successful leaders in economic life were therefore respected for their knowledge and judgment, and their views, when known, carried much weight. This was a perfectly natural result, which was evident even where there was no application of pressure or undue influence.

The situation that exists today in the large cities of the country is altogether different. The boss doesn't stop to chat with the night watchman about the local candidate for mayor, because the boss is no longer interested. Furthermore, if he expressed any views on the subject, they would be regarded with suspicion. Minor executives do not share with those under them any interests in the larger social relationships of the city, especially those of a political character, because all their interests of that kind are centered in the pink tea politics of some suburban community. The skilled workman at his bench has no feeling of community relationship with the superintendent who stops to inspect his work. This is the worst kind of cleavage along class lines. In effect, it produces mass frustration on the part of the average employees, and a feeling that their work is not a part of social living, but only a toilsome means to an unsatisfying end. They have no share in the community life of the suburban town, and are incapable of themselves exerting the leadership that would make their cities satisfactory and satisfying communities.

By voluntarily abdicating their community responsibilities, the leaders in business and their professions have left a leaderless proletariat in the great cities of the nation. Perhaps it would be more accurate to say that these millions were leaderless, for it is certainly no longer true that they lack "medicine men" to guide their social relationships. From the soapboxes, the sound trucks with their screeching phonographs, and over the radio come the exhortations of those leaders who are scrambling for the seats of power vacated by our suburban noblemen.

Of course, suburbanite executives will exclaim, "Surely there is no reason for us to stay in the city and suffer from conditions that we cannot control; and, horror of horrors, you would surely not advocate that our politically spotless suburb become a part of that misguided metropolis wherein we earn our daily bread?" However, to these suburbanites there is a sufficient answer, and it is: You will either fight these evils at home where you can come to grips with them, or be defeated by the results of your own abdication through a concentration of the powers that you deny the ability to handle separately.

The truth of the matter is that a nation wherein each man has a vote cannot long survive a division along class lines. It is precisely that type of classification that is being fostered and hastened by the growth of the American suburb. In a democracy, votes count, and as the masses rise to political power, they will not be long in stripping from our suburbanites the economic advantage that makes their fancied haven of refuge possible.

There are many things wrong in America, in the sense that they tend to disrupt orderly progress, and the chance for civilization's advancement. It would be silly to pretend that the city versus suburb class division was more than one of our serious problems. However, it is one that must sooner or later be faced by those who can do something, if they expect to pass on to their children something better than the unstable civilization that has been disturbing the peace of the nation with its economic sprees and headaches of the past few years. ❖

APPENDIX D

HOW TO CONTACT AIER

The American Institute for Economic Research is headquartered at 250 Division St., Great Barrington, Massachusetts, 01230. The mailing address is P.O. Box 1000, Great Barrington, Massachusetts, 01230. The phone number is (413) 528-1216.

The website URL is *aier.org*. Online visitors will find information about the Institute's history, research findings, publications, educational programs and job opportunities. Visitors also can access numerous articles on current economic affairs, and download many sample publications, such as John Dewey and Arthur Bentley's *Knowing and the Known*.

A special free feature on the website is the "Cost-of-Living Calculator" — an interactive, easy-to-use program allowing a person to calculate the present-day equivalent, in terms of purchasing power, of a dollar amount from any year since 1913. Another free feature is the "Loan Interest Calculator" — allowing a person to figure his or her monthly payment on a loan and discover how much interest — must be paid over the life of the loan.

To contact American Investment Services, an affiliate of the American Institute for Economic Research — which provides asset management and publishes the monthly *Investment Guide*, visit *americaninvestment.com* or call (413) 528-1216.

PHOTO INDEX

E.C. Harwood, U.S. Military Academy yearbook photo, 1920 XI

Life magazine cover, 1926 XII

Automobiles symbolized newfound wealth and increased mobility .XII

William James, American philosopher, psychologist and educator. .XV

Edward Harwood, age 3, with toy shovel and pail. XVII

Lt. Ed Harwood, first wife Harriet, daughter Midge, 1926 XVIII

E.C. Harwood with fellow high school student leaders, 1918 XIX

Lt. E.C. Harwood and horse, Hawaii XXI

President Franklin D. Roosevelt, at desk. 1

Men in soup line, New York, 1930s 2

Vannevar Bush, college administrator, scientist, inventor 2

Bank run, 1929. 3

Lt. E.C. Harwood, 1931, as associate professor at MIT. 8

Helen Fowle, as a young woman. 10

President Harry S Truman, at a press conference. 15

U.S. sailor kissing nurse in Times Square at news of Japan's surrender. 15

John Maynard Keynes at United Nations conference, 1944 16

Nuclear bomb test, Nevada Test Site 16

Edgewood, built by Frederick Stark Pearson. 20

Frederick Stark Pearson, 1910 21

Frederick Stark Pearson and family at Edgewood 22

Frederick Stark Pearson with prize-winning ram. 23

American family watches television, as in 1950s. 33

President Dwight D. Eisenhower at French cemetery. 33

1956 Ford Fairlane Victoria 34

Col. And Mrs. Harwood with four children, 1957. 36

Overhead view of the Institute's manor and grounds, 1955 37

Drummer and flutist at Woodstock music festival, 1969. 41

Astronaut plants U.S. flag on the moon 41

U.S. helicopters supporting ground troops in Vietnam 42

Dr. Martin Luther King Jr. and Malcolm X, 1964 42

Fred Harwood, Institute trustee. 46

E.C. Harwood with 11 grandchildren, 1967 49

E.C. and Helen Harwood at the Institute, 1965. 50

The Institute staff, 1962 51

Cars lined up at gas station during oil crisis, 1973 53

Disco party animals, 1970s 54

Campaign button for Jimmy Carter, 1976 54

Fortune Magazine photo of Col. Harwood, 1974. 62

Col. Harwood in front of San Salvatore Mountain, Switzerland. 63

Falçieu, in Switzerland — photo of long-term residences 64

Alpine setting for Falçieu 64

Front of Harwood Gold Piece. 68

Back of Harwood Gold Piece 68

Longtime Institute member Dr. Robert C. Weems. 70

President Ronald Reagan and First Lady Nancy. 75

New York Stock Exchange floor, 1980s 76

Col. Harwood, on 80th birthday, holding Swiss gold bar. 76

Helen and E.C. Harwood with daughter-in-law Michelle, 1971 79

Col. Harwood and son Fred, 1979 84

Rioters in Los Angeles following Rodney King case verdict, 1992 85

U.S. soldiers firing artillery before Kuwait invasion, 1990. 85

Computer expert with PC, 1980s 86

President Bill Clinton at press conference, 1999 86

Research fellow Walker Todd speaking at property rights conference, 2004 90

Dr. William Ford, visiting lecturer, 2007 92

Student fellow Christa Jensen, 2007 95

Research fellow Dr. Elaine Tan, 2007 98

Economist Anna Schwartz, speaking on the Euro 100

Walker Todd dropping lobster into pot 100

Student fellows playing volleyball 100

Student fellows relaxing at local restaurant on weekend 100

Student fellows at summer orientation, 2007 100

Student fellows saying goodbye at end of summer term, 2007 100

Property Rights Conference attendees, 2004 101

Geoff Hodgson, economics journal editor, presents at conference, 2007 101

Anna Schwartz checks the Euro's price in the *Wall Street Journal* 101

Institute staffers set up lights and video camera, 2007 101

Attendees pack auditorium during March 2007 conference 101

C. Lowell Harriss and Michael Rizzo, during 2006 summer session 102

Charles Murray and Dominic Salvatore, during 2007 summer session 102

Ernest Welker and Gerald Edelman at BRI conference, 2003 102

Nobel Prize-winner Gerald Edelman addresses BRI confab, 2003 102

Nobel Prize-winner Vernon Smith and John H. Wood, BRI confab, 2003 102

Smoke billows from World Trade Center towers, Sept. 11, 2001 103

Robert Gilmour, Institute president and CEO, 1991-2003 107

Charles Murray, Institute president and CEO 111

Institute director of research and education Kerry Lynch 115

Institute senior fellow Lawrence Pratt 117

Institute manager of facilities Bruce Gore 119

Longtime Institute employee Jean White, opening mail 122

Institute cook Linda Lis, at barbecue 123

Institute chief financial officer Shaun Buckler 123

Visitors gather on the Castle's patio 131

Rear view of the Castle 131

Exterior view of the Edward C. Harwood Library 131

Vista of the Berkshire Hills and Taconic Range. 131

Stretch of winding road leading from Division Street to the Institute. 131

View of Long Pond 131

Main hall of the Castle 132

First-floor TV room in the Castle 132

Circular staircase in the Castle. 132

Kitchen in the Castle 132

Guest room in the Castle. 132

The Institute's research library. 132

Roy Anderson Foulke, Sr., who chaired the Institute's board 139

Maureen Foulke, husband, Roy, Jr., son John and daughter Sarah. 140

Subject Index

American Institute Counselors (also AIC), 43, 49-51, 55-59, 61-62, 64, 68

American Institute for Economic Research (also AIER, and the Institute)
  book publisher, 133-137
  charitable giving, 137-138
  fellowship programs, XIII, 87-89, 91, 111, 137
  mission, XII, 130, 137, 139, 141
  move to Cambridge, 6-7, 79-80
  move to Great Barrington, 17-19, 22-23, 81
  1950s growth, 34-38
  origins, XI-XIII, 5-6, 79-80

American Investment Services (also AIS), 73-74, 117, 121, 140

Barron's, XV, XXI, 60

Behavioral Research Council (also BRC), 43-44

Bentley, Arthur, XV, 17, 44

Bush, George H.W., 75, 85

Bush, George W., 103

Bush, Vannevar, 5

Carter, Jimmy, 54-55, 75

the Castle, 23, 34, 47-48, 119, 121, 123

Clinton, Bill, 86

Coonley, Prentice, 22, 37-38

Cotswold, 22-23, 37-38, 56

Counsel of Economic Advisers, 33

Dewey, John, XV, XX, 17-18, 44, 47

dot-coms, 86-87, 103

Dow Jones Industrial Average (also Dow), XIII, 1, 33, 76-77, 86, 104

E.C. Harwood Library, 42, 88, 105, 119, 122

Economic Education Bulletins, XII, 28, 65, 105

Edgewood, 20-21

Falçieu, 50, 65

Federal Reserve, 8, 27, 77, 91, 93, 104, 113, 129, 166

Ford, Gerald R., 69

Ford, William F., 92-94

Fortune Magazine, 44, 62-63

Foulke, Maureen, 140-141

Foulke, Roy Anderson, Sr., 42, 139-141

Foulke, Roy Anderson, Jr. 140-141

Friedman, Milton, 69, 89

George, Henry, XV, XX

Gilmour, Robert, 107-110

gold
  investing in, 43-44, 46, 49-50, 55-56, 58, 60-65, 72, 82, 84
  standard, 3-4, 16, 47, 54, 58, 69, 82, 113

Gore, Bruce, 118-121

Great Depression (also Depression), XIII, XIV, XVI, 1, 3, 33, 105

Greenspan, Alan, 69, 129-130

gross national product (also: GNP), 34

Handy, Rollo, 44

Harriss, Lowell C., 89

Harwood, Edward Crosby (also E.C. Harwood,
Col. Harwood, the Colonel)

books authored, 8-9

childhood, XIV, XVII-XIX

"Down with the Radio, the Opiate of
the People," 150-151

early writing on economics, XV-XVI, 3-9,
11-14

education in economics, XIV-XV, XX-XXI

founding AIER, XI-XIII, XVI, 5

"The Full Significance of Freedom," 143-150

Harwood Gold Piece, 68

"The Investment Counselor Racket," 28-31

"The Menace of the American Suburb,"
151-155

obituaries, 82-84

"The Scientific Breakthrough of the
Twentieth Century," 38-39

"The Struggle Against Communism," 35

"Useful Procedures of Inquiry," 43

World War II service, 17-18, 80-81

Harwood, Eve, 47

Harwood, Fred, 28, 46-52, 78, 119, 143

Harwood, Helen Longfellow, XVIII, XX, 5-7,
9-11, 17-18, 22, 47, 51, 59, 120

"From Little Acorns," 78-81

obituary, 99

Harwood (Delay), Katherine, 47

Harwood, Kim, 52

Harwood, Kirk, 48. 52

Harwood, Michelle, 48, 52

Harwood, Midge, XXI

Harwood, Richard, XXI

Harwood, Ted, XXI

Harwood, William, 47, 51

Haynes (Harwood), Harriet, XX, XXI, 6

High Yield Dow, 117

Hoover, Herbert, 1

"How Inquiry Proceeds," 44-46

indicators (Leading, Coincident, Lagging), XII,
116, 118

inflation, XII, XXI, 5, 14, 24-28, 35-36, 46, 50,
52-54, 57-59, 63, 70-71, 75, 77, 85, 125, 137,
151-152

Internal Revenue Service (also IRS), XII, 42-43,
73, 139

James, William, XV, XX, 44

Jensen, Christa, 95-97

Johnson, Lyndon B., 42, 49

Kennedy, John F., 41

Keynes, John Maynard (also: Keynesian), 24-28,
33, 52-53, 58, 69, 71, 77

Korea (also Korean Conflict, Korean War), 34-
35, 48, 87

Lemnitzer, Lyman, 48

Lynch, Kerry, 115-116

Medicare, XII, 42, 104

Mondial Commercial Ltd., 44, 50-51, 61-63

Monte Sole, 50, 65

Murray, Charles, XI, 110-114

NASDAQ, 86-87, 103

New York Times, XXI, 68-69

Nixon, Richard M., 53-54

Pearson, Frederick Stark, 21

Peirce, Charles, 44

The Phoenix, 51, 81

Pratt, Lawrence, 112, 116-118

Progress Foundation, 43, 50, 55, 64-65, 130

Reagan, Ronald (also Reaganomics), 55, 75, 77

recession, XII, XVI, 3, 33, 75, 85, 116

Research Reports, XII, 6-7, 17, 47

    "A Cool Trillion," 125-127

    "A Starbucks a Day," 124-125

Roaring Twenties, XIII, XVI

Roosevelt, Franklin D., 1-3, 42, 77

S&P 500, 86, 125

Schwartz, Anna, 89, 91, 96

"The Scientific Procedures of Inquiry," 65-67

Securities and Exchange Commission (also SEC), XII, 3, 44, 50-51, 55-61, 140

Social Security, XII, 3, 59, 104

stagflation, 53

Switzerland, 43-44, 49-51, 55-60, 63, 65, 72

Tan, Elaine, 97-99

Todd, Walker, 90-92, 96-97, 113

Truman, Harry S, 16

Vietnam, 42, 48-49, 53

Wall Street Journal, 44, 60-61

Weems, Robert C., 70-73

White, Jean, 121-123

Zone 5 (marketing study), 105-106, 129-130